POLLBOOKS
HOW VICTORIANS VOTED

POLLBOOKS
HOW VICTORIANS VOTED

J. R. VINCENT
Fellow of Peterhouse, Cambridge

CAMBRIDGE
AT THE UNIVERSITY PRESS
1968

Published by the Syndics of the Cambridge University Press
Bentley House, 200 Euston Road, London, N.W.1
American Branch: 32 East 57th Street, New York, N.Y. 10022

Standard Book Number: 521 06712 X

Library of Congress Catalogue Card Number: 67–10160

First published 1967
Reprinted with corrections
1968

First printed in Great Britain at the University Printing House, Cambridge
Reprinted in Great Britain by William Lewis (Printers) Ltd, Cardiff

CONTENTS

PREFACE

This book is rather protean. The largest part of it is a compilation of data about voting in England in the nineteenth century, giving much material of which no use has been made here, but which might form a starting-point and source for others more acquainted with particular problems and localities. The introductory essay is concerned with the meaning of this heap of evidence, mainly at a rather general level. The traditional problem on which it chiefly throws light is the place of class in electoral politics—a problem better and more neutrally defined as one of the relation between the type of social situation a person is in, and his political outlook. It is on this question that discussion is concentrated.

The two concluding essays pursue the point from a different angle. The first analyses the social situation in Cambridgeshire in the middle of the nineteenth century, by using probate records, and suggests that the structure of capital ownership corresponded to certain distinctive features of contemporary political sensibility. The concluding essay ventures some thoughts on the change from Liberal to Labour, considered in terms of the function of politics in relation to the personal needs of the ordinary voter. The common thread uniting these fragments is a preoccupation with tracing political consciousness back to its roots in a personal situation, by yoking the surmises of sociological theory to empirical data gained from door-to-door interviews with the dead.

J.R.V.

ACKNOWLEDGEMENTS

The kindness of others has greatly assisted in the making of this book. Mr George Cunningham and the History of Parliament Trust have generously allowed me to draw on the fruits of their own researches into pollbooks. The compiler has also been able to draw on inquiries made by Mr N. P. Brecknell, Mr James Chadwick, and Miss Margaret Leslie, concerning Norwich, Dublin and Carlisle respectively. Miss J. Chambers gave stalwart assistance with some of the most burdensome work. Mr Brian Harrison drew my attention to some very interesting statistics which are referred to below. Dr Henry Pelling and Mr A. B. Cooke kindly brought to light certain highly relevant corrections and additions. I am greatly indebted to Miss C. A. Stoakley for the skill and care given to the typing of a difficult manuscript. All faults of conception and execution, however, stem peculiarly from the author.

I am very grateful to the Master and Fellows of Peterhouse who gave me the opportunity to do this work, and to the Trustees of the Twenty-Seven Foundation for a grant towards the cost of publication.

I

INTRODUCTION

1

Pollbooks are lists of voters at a given election, accompanied by indications of which candidate or candidates they voted for. This is the only feature common to all of them. (Lists of voters which do not state their votes exist fairly commonly in the form of electoral registers, and are of no use at all.) Most pollbooks were printed, but a few survive in manuscript. Most pollbooks were in pamphlet form, but some were weighty and expensive books, those for the West Riding for instance costing up to a pound. Most pollbooks give the address of the voter; but even this is not always to be found. Their internal arrangement varied considerably. Some grouped the voters by villages, wards, or even by streets. Others listed their names alphabetically, or according to the order of voting. Some distinguish between freemen electors and ten-pound householders, and between resident voters and out-voters: others make no such distinction. So far as can be seen, the jobbing printers who usually published pollbooks acted under no responsibility to anyone, and the consequences of their having had a free hand—sometimes good, sometimes bad—are evident in the complete lack of standard presentation in pollbooks. In a few cases pollbooks were published by political bodies, but in general everything depended on the free will of some small printer looking around for a small profit.

Hence there is little rhyme or reason in the distribution of places for which pollbooks were published, and the oddities which are most marked are those a historian would least desire. In times of political excitement, the printer had most incentive to publish a pollbook, and so the elections of the 1830s are very well represented. But when one turns to see what the new voters were doing in 1868, the pollbooks are taciturn, presumably because the great increase in the electorate would have made pollbooks too expensive to sell easily. The same considerations no doubt lay behind the absence of pollbooks for very large constituencies. No pollbook is known for Manchester after 1839, for Birmingham after 1841, or for any London seat after 1841. Everything depended, not on the social interest of the data, but on the chances of the printer recovering his costs.

Nevertheless, a very thorough search made by the History of Parliament Trust in 1953 revealed about 1,750 titles for England and Wales published over the whole period 1694–1872. The chances of a pollbook not surviving or, if surviving, of not having been found, are certainly high, but the figure of 1,750, including as it does all the titles in the handful of large collections, is a practical maximum. As an unsupported guess, one might say that a third to a half of all contested elections between 1830 and 1872 were reported in a printed pollbook.

Now all pollbooks might conceivably be made use of in relating party preferences to certain variables like occupations (taken from directories), wealth (taken from ratebooks), kinship (taken from the census), religious denominations (taken from congregational lists, if such exist), and the amount of savings possessed (taken from probate records).* Such investigations are conceivable and perhaps desirable, but for one person to try to find in such ways sufficient data to make generalizations at a national level, would be impossibly laborious.

It is fortunate therefore that a certain number of pollbooks give the occupations of those who voted. This kind of pollbook forms only a small fraction of the total, and therefore a still smaller fraction of all elections are described in this way. There are for instance no pollbooks giving voters' occupations for either Manchester or Birmingham. Nevertheless, where occupational pollbooks do exist, they enable one to relate party preference to that variable one would choose most to know about—occupation and social position —in a mechanical and exact, though still sufficiently laborious, way.

Nearly all the pollbooks between 1830 and the end of open voting in 1872 which give occupations of voters, are for borough constituencies, not for county seats. No county pollbook after 1852, to my knowledge, makes any pretence of stating occupations, and no county pollbook after 1835 does the job in a full and proper way. This is quite a lacuna, but it is not so important as the number of county seats would suggest. For on the one hand, the agricultural seats did not include as constituents the rich variety of human types found in the borough electorate: on the other hand, voting in the counties was much more related to the pattern of landownership and of traditional territorial influences than it was

* For a use of probate records on a local scale, showing at least the difficulty of deploying them, see ch. II below.

to occupation.* Analysis of the county vote by occupations would not be wrong exactly, but it would tell a very small part of the story. So the impossibility of such an analysis may be accepted with a good grace.

Most of the pollbooks which allowed analysis of voting by occupations have in fact been so analysed, and the results are set out in chapter III below. The few pollbooks which might have been analysed, and yet were not, were quite unimportant. Some elections in 1837, for instance, were omitted, when the same constituency had been analysed for 1835 or 1841. A few boroughs which were hopelessly corrupt or 'closed' were omitted. Some entirely one-sided elections where a freak candidate forced a poll, but with derisory results, were not worth considering. Some pollbooks in local libraries were too inaccessible to be worth a special journey. But the range of elections analysed below comes as near the maximum as it is worth while to go.

It may be objected that the range is too wide, that much of the material gathered below has no special interest, exhibits no striking features, and advances no great argument. This is undoubtedly true, and no one has felt this as much as the compiler. But in dealing with a new type of evidence, the defect of method which would be involved in reporting only 'interesting' results would much outweigh the gain in amenity. The world is quick enough to forget the existence and the importance of the merely amorphous, without doing its work for it.

It is not clear why some pollbooks give occupations and others do not. It may be a question of the balance between printers' costs and printers' pride in their work. Neither is it clear how the occupations got into the pollbooks at all—whether, for instance, some polling clerk wrote them down, and if so, how far he did so on his own ascriptions, and how far he accepted the self-assessment of the voter; or whether the printer himself added the occupations from common knowledge (possible only in a small town) or from street directories. The text for working purposes, then, is the text of the pollbook as it stands. One cannot, so to say, discern by internal evidence a 'historical election' standing behind what is reported to us, and make allowances accordingly. For the purposes of this book, pollbooks are texts which emerge *ex nihilo*, bearing

---

* For this point see D. C. Moore, 'The Other Face of Reform', in *Victorian Studies*, v (1961), and the analysis below of village block voting in the Lincoln-shire election of 1823.

within them, as will be seen, certain kinds of pragmatic verification, and so long as they are analysed as texts, rather than as historical realities, no question of methodological error arises.

Unfortunately no occupational pollbooks are known to exist for Bradford, Manchester, Birmingham, Salford, Liverpool after 1841, Norwich after 1830, Bristol after 1852, Portsmouth, or any of the London constituencies at any date between 1830 and 1872. The bias is strongly towards the medium-sized constituency of 10,000 to 50,000 people, normally a market, county, or cathedral town rather than a manufacturing centre, which was in any case the central element in the English electoral system. The pollbooks throw little light on the politics of great cities, of the Industrial Revolution, on the tendencies which rose to importance chiefly after 1872, and this is a pity so far as knowledge of political behaviour goes. But their bias in this respect is really rather salutary, as it corresponded to the actual bias and weighting of the electoral régime. It brings one nearer to the actual social structure and economic life of the country, to Dickens' England, than an attention to the precocities of Lancashire would.

2

The question now arises what kinds of inquiry are and are not advanced by the occupational analysis of party preferences. There is also a third group of topics, to which the tables below are relevant, but no particular effort has been made in this work to develop the data incidentally included there. Among this third group are such questions as which occupations tended to vote for persons, which for parties; which respected legitimate traditional influences most; which occupations changed proportionately to the electorate between 1832 and 1865; and what the effect of the Reform Bills of 1832 and 1867 was on the social balance of a constituency. For example, a comparison of the Cambridge pollbook of 1866 with that of 1868 brings out exactly the effect of Reform on the constituency. On these and other topics, the tables given below will probably be found to have something to say: and their extensive publication may be worth while in this respect, as a work of reference, reaching no conclusions itself, for others to quarry from.

Even in some questions of electoral politics, pollbooks are a broken reed, and the method of occupational analysis the wrong method. For precisely as it is well suited to the analysis of the main structure and substance of political behaviour, so is it ill suited to the analysis of contingencies, events, and small fluctuations. Of course it is very useful in giving quantity and social locality to the eruption of Reform in 1830-2, but it is an insensitive instrument for recording political changes in the very evenly balanced 'normal' elections between 1835 and 1872, let alone for interpreting them. Pollbooks are not much use for writing a history of the course of events at national level. Detailed analysis of many constituencies of much the same type, in order to derive the fate of a nation, an election, or a constituency from some final inconsequence or loose end, is hardly a step forward from leaving the causes of the ups and downs of Victorian elections as undefined and anecdotal as at present. Perhaps when a more systematic approach than argument by the accumulation of instances has been adopted in the study of general elections, the tables below may come to illustrate, what they cannot now demonstrate. 'The need is not so much for more studies of...constituencies, as for a classification of the range of constituencies, followed by studies of sample constituencies of widely differing characteristics.'* The analyses of individual constituencies given below do not pretend to have the usefulness that a quantitative typology of constituencies would have for the writing of the history of events.

Since knowledge of Victorian political behaviour has hitherto been nearly entirely qualitative, not to say anecdotal, it is hardly necessary to apologize for the omissions inherent in a quantitative study. Numbers do not record fervour, and they do not directly record effort, a rather different quality. (It must be remembered that corruption is the obverse of somebody else's zeal, organizing skill, and financial sacrifice.) The excitement which men were feeling over a particular burning issue appears in the tables only in the form of some general occupational tendency to prefer one party to another. And so on: the losses and gains of such matters are well rehearsed. Apology is needed more for statistical omissions than for statistical excesses. The voting of clerical personnel and contemporary literature all suggest the immense importance of religious denomination for political and indeed for every kind of behaviour. It would therefore be very useful to relate party preference among the laity to religious denomination. But unfortunately there is no royal road here as there is with occupations. In certain fortunate cases the relation might be worked out on a small scale,

* H. J. Hanham, *Political Studies* (1955-6), p. 151.

B

though the results would be hard to obtain and probably, owing to the duplication of common names, rather inaccurate.

The question of the relation between voting and wealth, as shown either in the ratebook or in probate records, was not nearly so insuperable on the technical side, but it was much more superfluous. For occupation, taken by and large, gives an implicit and politically sufficient assessment of wealth, without taking the matter further by inquiries into the means of actual individuals. The divergence between rich and poor shoemakers, for instance, may have been quite considerable, both as regards fortune and as regards politics: but it was as nothing compared with the difference between shoemakers in general, and gentlemen in general.

Though their fortunes might vary considerably upward or downward, all shoemakers shared in a body of social opinion about what kind of people shoemakers were, which in turn derived from an objective economic homogeneity* natural to skilled small producers competing in a free market. Shoemakers were poor enough to feel poor, or to be felt to be poor by others, and they were rich enough to feel independent, or to want to be so. Nevertheless, studies of probate records may have much to add, if they can show, what one suspects, that the capital and savings of skilled non-factory workers and small shopkeepers were high, relatively both to their own earnings, and to the savings/income ratio† of skilled factory workers or unskilled workers then and now. This would be a convenient conclusion, for it would bring together many hints that the 'people' in the towns were, in economic type and in political psychology, not proletarians selling their labour on the market, but something closer to the peasant type than English rural conditions had allowed in most parts of the country for some time. Urbanization, Dr Kitson Clark has succinctly said, preceded mechanization, and in this one fact there is a world of political consequences. It would do much to explain the reverence for property—so long as it was small property—in Radical oratory and

---

* See ch. II below.

† Working-class savings now are probably low in relation to annual income: see the recent studies by the Acton Society, *Acton Survey of Manual Workers' Savings Habits and Attitudes to Share Ownership* (1965) which found that over one-third of workers interviewed had under £50 saved; and by Dorothy Wedderburn, *Redundancy and the Railwaymen* (1965), which found that 54 per cent of the workers interviewed said they had no savings at all, and another 10 per cent said they had less than £50, whereas only 25 per cent claimed to have over £100.

practice. It would make less puzzling the resemblance between French and English radicalism in the later nineteenth century, if both arose from a similar economic type of small producer and proprietor, mainly urban in England, mainly rural in France. The ethic of thrift, too, came from a lower social level than that of businessmen, from a kind of poor person who was as, or more, concerned about his capital than about his income, unlike the proletarian to whom capital is an accidental and rather functionless surplus from income. As a working hypothesis which at least fits a number of phenomena which would otherwise be puzzling, it may therefore be suggested that while the Industrial Revolution produced proletarians in some factory districts (and these were often the wives and children of men* engaged as independent producers in non-factory work), over the country in general the economic growth with which it was associated worked for quite a long time in favour of a wider distribution of small property and a diminution of the relative power of large property (for which in the towns an institutional framework, such as the industrial joint stock company, and an economic *raison d'être* were alike lacking). Hence the emergence of Liberalism, which had always been endemic in the social strata now given that strength which was all they had ever needed.

We are left with three present and solid objects to pursue for which the method of occupational analysis is quite suitable. The first is the provision of miscellaneous information about voting behaviour of strictly limited significance—about the existence of anomalies, archaisms, pressure groups, economic and local interests, and institutionally, ecclesiastically, or educationally shaped voting. The second object is to test traditional explanations or descriptions of political behaviour in the light of the facts given by occupational analysis. Thirdly and more positively, it is then reasonable to try to construct a general description, which will also be partly an explanation, of voting behaviour inductively, by grouping many minute particulars into a few typical probabilities or ratios of voting preference. Having arrived at a general account of the

---

* English cotton operatives in 1871:

	under 20	over 20
Male	69,996	118,276
Female	118,602	161,268

(G. Phillips Bevan, *The Industrial Classes and Industrial Statistics* (1876), p. 7.)

phenomena, it is then possible to check against it some of the various possible ideas of class, to see whether these ideas have either factual value or explanatory insight.

3

The difficulties of interpreting pollbooks come under two heads. On the one hand it has to be asked whether one is arranging accurate data in an intelligent way. On the other hand, it has to be asked whether the votes given, though accurately recorded and collected, are empty of the kind of meaning they would need to have to be sociologically useful—either because, though freely given, the votes had no general significance for the person who gave them, or because votes often represented the wishes of anyone but the voter.

> I am his Highness' dog at Kew.
> Pray tell me Sir, whose dog are you?

The accuracy of the data cannot be checked against the anterior reality of which it is a recension. But strong checks for internal consistency and inherent probability can be applied, from which pollbooks emerge with flying colours. First there is a reasonable congruence between the numbers and preferences of the various occupations in successive elections in the same town. Secondly, the results of occupational analysis do not conflict with the general direction of traditional knowledge, they only strengthen or dilute it. Church and chapel, rich and poor, as recorded in the pollbooks, never vote in ways that outrage one's sense of reality. Thirdly, where there are two candidates on each side, their voting can be shown to differ only where electoral reason says it ought to: e.g. the Leicester publicans voted Liberal in general, but abstained point blank from supporting a Liberal Temperance candidate. Fourthly, there was no motive for falsification except laziness, and still less for the falsification of group voting, which would not be apparent to the reader of the pollbook. Fifthly, certain consistent national patterns do emerge from pollbook after pollbook. Such pragmatic justifications cannot prove the accuracy of any particular pollbook on any particular detail—this just cannot be done—but they do suggest that broad generalizations may safely be made from large collections of these figures, each one of which taken alone would be entirely open to question.

The figures in the pollbooks are probably usually accurate in detail and taken as a whole they are self-validating. The question is how to use them meaningfully. This depends on the choice of occupational categories, on the homogeneity of the categories chosen, and on the statistical significance of voting variations in fairly small groups of people. The actual definitions of the occupations used are given in the note in chapter II below. So long as only some and not all occupations were tabulated, inaccuracy of a kind was bound to arise, since no occupations were exactly typical of some general group of occupations. The operative question, however, is whether a selective analysis of occupations led to special rather than marginal inaccuracies, and this can be largely answered by looking at the few constituencies (e.g. Ashton, Bedford, Rochdale) where every occupation was analysed, and noting the degree of correspondence between the 'typical' occupation selected (e.g. grocers, shoemakers) and the stratum to which it belonged (Craftsmen, Retailers).

No assumptions are made in this study about the homogeneity of the occupations analysed. It would make for smoothness of argument if people of the same occupation corresponded to a certain stratum of society and were in much the same circumstances. This was no doubt often so. Small producers and small shopkeepers competing under conditions of free entry tend to a general equality of condition, and the few big shops in the High Street, which would be politically influential, were submerged in elections by the 'average' grocer in the ubiquitous corner shop. On the other hand, some occupations like the clergy and officers were distinctly vertical, hierarchical groups, and a curate at the bottom might earn much less than a farm labourer with an employed family. The idea that occupation as analysed below corresponded generally to fairly homogeneous horizontal strata may be a cornerstone of one's imaginative understanding of the situation, but it cannot be derived from exact knowledge.

Many of the figures given in the tables below are small: mostly below 30, many below 10. Can such low numbers really show any meaningful tendency? They certainly can where they are meant to, but often they are not meant to. Where a very few railwaymen, farmers, or weavers are listed, this is not because their voting is thought to provide evidence for the political behaviour of such people in general, but is intended simply as a convenient reminder that these people were not important in this election. The number of bankers in each town was very small, and their party preferences as measured below simply record whether one banking family was larger than another. However, by addition of evidence from many towns, one can draw general conclusions about the politics of bankers. They were in fact quite Liberal—at least as much so as the labourers—which was to say nothing extravagant, but something very different from the position of bankers after 1880.

With clergy and dissenting ministers, who were necessarily sparsely distributed, very small numbers in each locality accumulate nationally to give a very strong indication of party preference. With normal secular groups, however, a high degree of significance is reached only when there is a fairly sharp preference within groups of at least 30 people. In Rochdale for instance the butchers voted Tory in 1857 by 25 to 16. The chances against this result being purely accidental would be about 500 to 1, according to the binomial theorem. The real difficulties in the tables below lie in determining what meaning, if any, the votes given had, not in their potentialities as statistical material.

Corruption and influence may affect the occupational analysis of political preference in five ways. Occupational analysis, at the very least, can show the incidence and social locality of corruption, if indeed a separate class of corrupt votes existed. A second possibility is that even in general corrupt conditions, an underlying genuinely political preference may shine through against all that gold and influence could do. The Norwich and Beverley elections are perhaps cases of this. Thirdly, corruption may on balance have coincided with a genuine preference by voters, and simply have intensified or revealed what was always latent. Fourthly, much of the less flagrant pressure on voters had nothing to do with open voting or the special conditions of Victorian England, but simply represented the irreducible tendency for genuine political preferences to be shaped by the situation in which people find themselves, and especially by the more important people within their daily horizon. This would be as important now as then.

Fifthly, it is possible that external influences completely obliterated the will and intention of great sections of voters, and that no conclusions, except as to proneness to corruption, can be reached from their votes. In the extreme case of servants, it must readily be admitted that the voting of servants should be understood as a double vote for their employers.* (Servants in fact rarely voted

* E.g. the voting of servants at Preston in 1830.

before 1868.) Yet in all other cases, it is doubtful whether influence alone controlled any important group of urban voters. The Toryism of Cambridge college servants, for instance, however agreeable to their employers, can plausibly be seen as coincident with a real political preference.

Only on the most extreme hypothesis, therefore, does corruption and influence nullify the value of occupational analysis. So far as electoral results went, in the period of political balance corruption probably decided the day very often. But it did not touch the core of political behaviour. In fact limits, social and geographical, can be set to the extent of corruption. Manchester and many larger towns never produced a clear case, and this although there was a great incentive for the losing side to get up a petition. Lawyers and publicans were bought, under face-saving conventions, and labourers and the waterfront population expected their due. But money had to flow pretty freely—as at Preston—before small shopkeepers would take the risk of voting against the non-monetary pressures of kin, denomination, and customers. Open voting and small town opinion created its own safeguards against people being lured away from the ruts into which they were born, into doing things they did not really agree with. The evidence of election petitions cuts both ways:

I think you find Norwich to be this: that you would find on the one hand, amongst the general class of voters, a very large class of partisans most anxious to do all they can to assist the candidates and their cause at the slightest expense, taking a most enormous lot of trouble, and never thinking of asking for a farthing of remuneration; whilst another class will take all they can get...one half would labour without the slightest remuneration for the most intense hard work.*

Another important point in suggesting a limited view of the importance of corruption, not in determining election results, but in determining political behaviour generally, is that though the relative will and power of each party to buy votes varied enormously from election to election and from candidate to candidate, the patterns of occupational preference remain relatively stable from year to year and from one place to another. Croesus fought many elections, but he never made shoemakers into good Tories, or butchers into good Liberals. Again, some electoral patterns are very hard to ascribe to influence. In many cases the rich or the

* *Parl. Papers* 1852–3, H.C. 243, q. 517 (Norwich Election).

employers in a town were fairly evenly divided, yet those beneath them showed sharp preference one way or the other. *A fortiori*, cases (like the Rochester bargees in 1868), where men vote strongly against the influential people closest in contact with them, are most likely to arise from genuine feeling.

Corruption means that any case of occupational preference in a particular election has to be treated with caution unless one is unusually well informed as to the local circumstances. But when one finds a pattern recurring in different elections in different places, then corruption can almost be forgotten about. There is a partial exception to this, however. This is because the Tories, especially after 1860, had the advantage in money, both centrally and in most localities, and therefore the Tory vote among labourers, shopkeepers, publicans, and craftsmen has to be construed with one eye on corruption. But this Tory vote existed—possibly only from habit—even at the most apparently pure elections, and there are many other, less adventitious, explanations for popular Toryism.

What of the vote which, though freely given, means nothing to the man who gives it? Mindlessness is perhaps a constant in political behaviour. But in 1850, probably more than now, the world was full of sharp reminders for the thriving earthworm that politics existed. There was a popular political culture as there was a popular musical culture, and the urban voter lived in packed and noisy streets where things happened. Very high polls,* very strict voting for a party ticket in the two-member seats, and broken windows bear witness to the strongly and consciously political intent of the electorate.

Nevertheless, often the vote given must have borne no relation to the man or his life, or have been entirely unconnected with any general political feeling. So be it. One can only hope that this kind of vote, which is an empty box, is evenly enough distributed among each group and party to make no difference.

* The county council elections in Cheshire can be cited to illustrate the difference between the modern and the nineteenth-century sense of mass involvement. The average poll in contested seats in the first two elections was over 70 per cent. In two cases a poll of 89 per cent was recorded, and polls under 50 per cent were almost unknown in county council elections before 1914. At the 1946 election, on the other hand, the average poll in contested seats was only 31·8 per cent. Sources: John M. Lee, *Social Leaders and Public Persons: A Study of County Government in Cheshire since 1888* (1963), pp. 53, 165. Cf. the high turnout of 94 per cent at the Lancaster election of 1865, below.

4

Pollbooks provide much information which is either pure detail or
else can only be generalized at a very low level. For instance, the
sweeps of Cambridge, Maidstone (1870), and Ipswich, perhaps
personally affronted by reforming legislation, all voted Tory in the
1860s, and there is an end to the matter. Other kinds of detail,
however, can be grouped and brought to focus on hypotheses.
There is only room here to discuss the light thrown by the tables
of voting on the relation between occupation and party preference,
but it should not be overlooked that much else may be illustrated
from them. For instance, the tables can show the effect of enfranchisement in 1832* and 1868 on the size and nature of the
constituencies (see especially the tables for Cambridge, 1866 and
1868). It can show, in the great crisis of 1830–2, which parts of
society were the moving, which the yielding, and which the resist-
ing part. The *non possumus* of the clergy, for example, in the great
debate comes out very clearly in the tables for Northamptonshire,
Hertfordshire, and Cambridge University. This in turn bears on
the interpretative crux on the first Reform movement—whether
Reform was egoistic or altruistic, conceded or taken, wisely
yielded by the influential, or harshly grasped by the uninfluential.
(The second Reform crisis does not show up in the pollbooks, as
the general elections of 1865 and 1868 were not fought on this
question.) But much else lies latent in the tables following, which
I do not now seek to elicit: the social location of the floating vote,
in constituencies where a long run of elections have been analysed;
the convention by which both Tories and Radicals, in many small
boroughs, as at Tamworth and Chichester, voted both for their
own candidate, and for the nominee of a (probably Whig) aristocratic patron; the pressure of appearances which brought many
professional men, especially in Liverpool, to split their votes between the more popular candidates on each side; and the degree
of correspondence in votes polled between candidates of the same
party, an important indicator of ill-disguised social cleavages, and
enlightening as to whether people voted for the party label or for
the man. These matters, which concern more the patterns of
voting peculiar to an occupation, rather than its party preference,

* For a comparative view of the preferences of old and new voters after the first
Reform Act, see the tables for the Huntingdon election of 1832, and the
Ipswich election of 1835.

are not intended to be specially exhibited in the tables, though these must necessarily include much information about them.

About certain occupations, there is little information. Coal miners appear in force only in Bristol in 1841 and in Shropshire in 1832, in both cases as Liberals. The only agricultural labourers recorded are those dismally Tory villagers who voted in the Leicester borough elections. The silk industry is represented only by the Lancaster election of 1865, where the silk interest voted Liberal by 17 to 4, despite the adverse effects of free trade on the silk industry. The many farmers whose votes are analysed, including an unexpected number in Oldham and Leeds, give no idea really as to the state of agricultural politics and the influence of landlords. We are left with three types of constituency about which there is sufficient information to build up a typical picture: viz. (1) the northern industrial town like Ashton, Warrington, Bolton, or Rochdale; (2) the provincial metropolis like Bristol, Norwich, Liverpool, Glasgow, or Leeds; (3) the cathedral, market, or county town of medium size and traditional economic character like Ipswich, Maidstone, or Cambridge. (The East Midlands towns of Leicester, Northampton and Nottingham combined features of all three types.) The problems and hypotheses which follow relate to widespread voting habits, which stand quite apart from the general grounds of political orientation on the one hand, but are yet so obviously structural as to require a sociological explanation. These are (1) the effect on the boroughs of rural intrusions from the Conservative countryside; (2) the relation between the party preference of a retailer or artisan and the typical social status of his customers; (3) the existence of an anomalous Toryism among the seafaring and longshore population of great ports; (4) the existence of an anomalous Toryism among labourers in boroughs; (5) the conflict between the drink trade and some Liberals; (6) the conflict between Church and Chapel; (7) the effect of higher education on party preference; and (8) the use of minor public employees and officials for party purposes. The type of conflict involved here takes place essentially within a situation of small scale; it is not conflict about the structure of the national political and economic order, though in some cases, for instance Church and Chapel, an apparently 'horizontal' conflict between competing interests was really the *alter ego* of dispute about the whole national society.

One line of division between the parties in the boroughs lay in the tendency of the Liberals to represent the essence and core of the town—business, shopkeeping, and craftsmanship—the general self-esteem of the townspeople, and their social ethic and common culture while the Tories, the minority party, were a coalition of 'outs', of those who could not quite be fitted in, operating under the hegemony of the outside forces of the countryside, as a fifth column within the gates of bourgeois Liberalism. The lawyers, doctors, coachbuilders, clergy, schoolmasters, architects, saddlers, wine merchants, butchers, jewellers, bookbinders, artists, and hatters, who looked for reward in higher quarters than from mere townspeople, appear in the pollbooks as epiphenomena of a mainly Tory landed ruling class, as a sort of upper servants. No disrespect is intended to their sincerity. It was simply a question of how far the pattern of their lives wove them into, or set them apart from, the mass of the borough population. Law, in particular, was an urban industry dependent on rural raw material, and the voting of lawyers in such county towns as Wakefield and Norwich marks this well, they being far to the right of the upper class in general there. (In Norwich, the solicitors nearly monopolized the local Tory leadership.) The pollbooks offer much evidence of the intrusive pressure of rural influences in market, cathedral, and county and to a lesser extent in some provincial capitals like Bristol or Norwich.

There are considerable and sociologically significant differences in voting of different kinds of craftsmen and shopkeepers, mostly along the lines one would expect. In Bolton, Preston in 1841, and Rochdale, for instance, cloggers, who sold only to the poorest, were entirely radical, while shoemakers, themselves little better off than cloggers, but selling to all kinds of persons, were more mixed in opinion. Beersellers, who chiefly served the dregs of society, were normally significantly more radical than publicans, who hoped for more catholic congregations. The difficulty here lies not in the evidence being unsympathetic to basing the voting of shopkeepers on the social position of those they sought to supply, but in the existence of alternative explanations. For, even setting aside the difference between emporium and corner shop within the single trade, there is great variation in economic position of the average of each trade. It is impossible to distinguish how much the Toryism of wine merchants (like Ruskin's father) depended on their own substantial stake in society, and how much rubbed off from a · Tory clientele. The point remains, that in most boroughs the shopkeepers are radical, by a good deal less than two to one, and that they and the craftsmen provide the backbone of the Liberal vote; but that politically they are internally divided along a line running from completely Jacobin sympathies, to complete identification with the 'county', this gradation being governed less by what they think they think, than by their kind of customers and their own position. The two latter criteria tended to go together (chemists are a case in point). The exception lies in the case of the butchers and grocers, the single stark revelation these inquiries have produced. Over generations, Tory butchers have been locked in combat with Radical grocers: the statistics are beyond doubt: but of this, no explanation, no word of description even, has come down to us. It is easy to form conjectures as to the reason for such a schism in the High Street, once one knows of it; but more salutary to reflect, how little one's stock ideas could have enabled one to predict this homely fact *ex ante*.

In the ports of Liverpool and Bristol, while the carpenters, cobblers, and shopkeepers were as radical as elsewhere, the shipwrights, mariners, pilots, sailmakers, and so on, constituted practically a bloc vote on the Tory side. Traces of the same thing may be found at Ipswich, Hull (possibly), and in some Kentish ports. Everywhere the pilots seem to be under some Tory spell.* To all appearances, there was a militant Tory working-class community down by the docks, and an equally militant radical working class—capable, be it remembered, of the very effective Bristol riots of 1831—among the artisans and shopkeepers of the landward districts. This was no case of a 'popular' Tory party acting as the means of conflict with a Liberal business oligarchy (party names differing but the conflict being the same) but something falling outside the category of class explanation entirely. To some extent, conflict arose from interests, such as the West Indies trade and the Navigation Laws, which were put in jeopardy by the Liberals. But the duration and depth of this deviation suggest something more chthonic—a separate sense of identity, hereditary solidarity, and a closed world of experience—acting to turn a temporary perception about material advantage, into a lasting political habit.

There is also much evidence of a less deep-seated, but more widespread, tendency for labourers in towns to vote Tory rather than Liberal, and to vote less Liberal than the craftsmen and shopkeepers, on the occasions when they did vote Liberal. In the towns for which this category was analysed, there were 41 elections in

---

* Except at Sandwich in 1868.

which the leading Tory candidate received more votes than the leading Liberal, against 20 cases where he received less. Disraeli's idea of an untapped Tory stratum lying beneath middle class radicalism had a certain amount of justification over the period 1832–68, though it should be noticed that in 1868, where there were many labouring voters, as at Cambridge, they were radical. Before 1868, the Toryism of the labourers is largely accounted for by their fewness and their corruptibility, but sometimes there is rather more to it than that. For instance, why should the Maidstone papermakers have voted Liberal by 2 to 1 from 1857 to 1865, while the Maidstone labourers were Tory? First, the condition of life of labourers did not permit the kind of radical political consciousness which required literacy and some leisure; secondly, labourers were in frequent contact with the less amiable face of the lower middle class and the labour aristocracy. At some points, e.g. over limitation of, and premiums on apprenticeship, the radical élite met the labourers in something like class war; at all points, they met as foreign bodies with distinct fates and without fraternity.* The Tory vote among the labourers, originating in contingencies, chance attachments and pressures, had by 1868 hardened into a deep-rooted habit, rationalized by better explanations than the genetic one.

The pollbooks do not show the social location of the Temperance vote, though this undoubtedly existed as such in the great provincial cities in the 1860s. They do, however, show the operation of the drink trade as a pressure group from the late 1850s onward, not indeed uniformly, but only where the Liberal candidate was thought to be 'dry'. Examples are the Rochdale election of 1857, and the Leicester elections of 1859 and 1861, where the publicans boycotted the Temperance Liberal, J. D. Harris, while still voting for the other Liberal candidates. It is possible, too, that the Beer Bill of 1830 had some effect in throwing the trade behind Reform; the liberalism of the trade in Liverpool in 1832 is surprisingly marked. The trade can also be found rallying round Liberal members who were its lobbyists in Parliament, like Berkeley at Bristol. What matters most for national history, is the vigorous *ils ne passeront pas* with which the trade met the

* There was 'a certain understood dignity and exclusiveness of caste pertaining to the artisan class which every individual of it is compelled to respect and support. A mechanic when out of work can scarcely take work as a labourer, even if it is offered him' (Thomas Wright, 'A Journeyman Engineer', *Some Habits and Customs of the Working Classes*, 1867, p. 258).

Temperance movement. This was a perfect example of a pressure group—a sharply defined group of people organized to defend their economic interest by rational electoral pressure, uninvolved in general political issues and without ideological overtones. What is remarkable is that the drink trade is perhaps the only interest, apart from the Catholic Church, which really operated in this way. There is no sign at all in the pollbooks that beneath the 'conventional issues of politics' one can find an earthy 'reality' consisting of the mutual pressures of rationally egoistic small-scale groups. The explanatory value of the idea 'pressure group' in electoral politics is negative, as indicating how political opinions were *not* normally formed. In the case of the publicans, their conviviality, their established trade societies, their training in reality, all fitted them to react to the unfairness of the Temperance threat in a cool, utilitarian, effective way. Their behaviour was not distinguished only in Victorian politics: for it is unusual anywhere for a lower middle-class group, faced with an appalling threat to its livelihood, to react by turning to intelligent manipulation of the traditional party system, rather than revolting against the system altogether.

Many things, at first classifiable as pressure groups, are really special cases deriving from a more general conflict. Thus at Bristol, the local struggle of the West India interest (the clergy supporting slavery) coincided with the general contest between the forces of order and the scruffier elements of society. Likewise one can trace in the conflict of Church and Chapel how education and tradition can harden a broad, but hardly imperative, division of interests, into a quite rigid difference of political culture. No other occupation was so partisan, so militant, so unfloating, as the Dissenting ministers. They were a sort of Communist hard core to the Popular Front. (Incidentally, the traditional impression that Wesleyan ministers were Tory is not borne out by the limited evidence so far found.) Moreover, clerical militancy was as great in Manchester (1839) as in rural areas like Suffolk or in the old county towns. Conversely, the voting of Anglican clergy, sextons, organists, and gravediggers was more unevenly split between the parties, by a long way, than was the voting of the most reactionary or the most revolutionary secular occupation.

Higher education had, in lesser degree, the effect of ecclesiastical employment in sharpening party preference. To some extent the issues merge, since so much of higher education was an Anglican preserve. However, the upper crust was broadly divided within itself on an educational basis which did not obviously correspond to economic or social inequalities. The Liberal professions were most likely to be Tory: the gentlemen, *soi disant*, were usually fairly evenly split; and the business world was inclined to be Liberal, though not by very much. This corresponds fairly well with the differing degrees of education endured by each type.

The serious reader will find no theoretical meat in the frequent instances given of the politics of bumbledom. Policemen, lamplighters, turnkeys, beedsmen, pilots, firemen—the preferences of these belong only to the curiosities of literature and the malpractices of Conservative electioneering, so far as individual cases are concerned. Not that what happened could cause anything but grave suspicion: the postmen of Shrewsbury in 1868, the pilots everywhere and always, the turnkeys in county towns like Cambridge, Lewes, Leicester, and especially Maidstone, at election after election, behaved so as to suggest that public authority, somewhere along the line, was turned to private use. But taking these contingencies as a whole into account, a point of some importance surely emerges: that, even on a cursory inspection, a wide range of occupations can be found, in which institutional influences caused a marked deviation from the pattern of voting normal to that condition of life in general. This deviation was normally in the direction of the Tories, but in all cases it produced a much more marked affiliation to one or other party than would otherwise have been the case. The institutional structure of borough or county injects a tincture of exact and socially determined opinion into the general welter of merely mental opinion, so to say, with the result that, through the growth and connection of families and changes of employment and home, any strong and exact body of opinion formed in one part of the polity must dissolve and diffuse and multiply till it colours a fraction at least of all parts of society. This is the permanent countervailing process, on the animal and ecological side, which ensured that in no section of society did the preference for one party over another rise to a very high ratio.

In conclusion, let us point to three details which may be cherished, as bearing on the proverbial side of human character. At Rochester* in 1868, all the bargemasters voted Liberal, and all the bargees Tory. At Cambridge, the college servants voted Tory

---

* At Rochester, in the same election, the eight postmen voted Liberal, while the postmaster voted Tory.

in season and out of season. It is still more agreeable to find that the Roman Catholic clergy, in the age of Newman and Pio Nono, swallowed their principles and voted almost solidly Liberal.* Here, as with the publicans, calculation quite overlaid feeling, showing the successful function of parties in creating agreement on immediate action, between fundamentally irreconcilable groups—and the Catholics and the Nonconformists in the Liberal rank and file were never far from coming to blows. Party is a civilizing thing: it has to unite many people, and overcome many conflicts, before it can even begin to be divisive in turn itself.

5

The evidence gleaned from the pollbooks may serve to modify some prevailing impressions. In the first place, in all types of town and city, the electorate was predominantly involved in pre-industrial types of activity. Even in Ashton, a cotton town *pur sang*, only a sixth of voters were connected with the cotton industry. The rank and file of both parties was drawn to an almost equal extent from the lower middle class and the aristocracy of labour. The suburban genteel vote did not exist. The *primum mobile* of the Liberal party, in particular, was generally popular, in the sense of coming from the *menu peuple*, not from an ascendancy of employers and captains of industry, nor from proletarian masses working in factories. The business and professional classes were numerically small and half assimilated to the upper crust, and a long way below these come what one can only call 'the people', who comprised the great majority of politically articulate people in any town, and who combined working-class and middle-class characteristics. There are, then, only two great substantial classes, 'the people' and 'the upper crust', to take into account; and each party was strong in each class. Parties may have had their genesis in class, and their function may have been to meet class needs, but the correlation between class membership and party preference, though positive, was too slight to have been of any predictive value for any particular group, occupation, locality, or person.

The business community was not a coherent entity, and it was not especially committed to middle-class liberalism. It is necessary to be quite specific as to what kind of business is meant, at what time and place. In Wakefield, the ironfounders and worsted spin-

* Cf. the Liverpool election of 1835 for the Liberal vote of the only Rabbi recorded below.

ners tended to be Tory, the woolstaplers and manufacturers Liberal. In Warrington, in 1847, cotton was entirely Liberal, but the industry of the town as a whole was evenly divided. At Warwick, in 1831, the woollen interest supported reform by 23 votes to 1, while at Preston, in 1841, the manufacturers were divided equally between the parties, and their overlookers were Tory by a ratio of 3 to 2. In the East Midlands, the manufacturers were primarily conscious of being in conflict with the great landowners of the surrounding countryside, and thus retained their pristine virtue, e.g. the lace manufacturers of Nottingham in 1852 were Liberal by 2 to 1. But in towns like Liverpool and Bristol, the business community, less conscious of domination by the territorial aristocracy, and reacting against the popular radicalism of the 1830s, played the part of a 'force of order'. On the whole, the textile employers of Lancashire and the East Midlands were Liberal; the business and mercantile communities of the great provincial capitals, divided evenly, or became Tory in anxious times; and the small family businesses—builders, millers, and so on—of the market towns were Liberal. Whatever the exact formula may be, England never lacked Tory businessmen.

One of the most amiable innuendos in English history is the suggestion that political change was achieved through the enlightenment of the rich; that, in the happy days 'before the rise of Socialism', the rich were reasonably progressive in the narrow party sense, and that the educated among them in particular led the way forward to a better and higher state of things. Now in the narrow party and electoral sense, this is not really so. Political change was achieved by popular electoral ascendancy over a recalcitrant upper crust. Liberalism genuinely had to contend against a great weight of 'soundness', and, considering political orientation only and not policy, the victory of the people over their betters at the polls was the necessary cause of Victorian Liberalism. If I am led to state this somewhat stridently, it is because a certain school of persons, who never fail to refer to Gradgrind, have thought fit to argue that Victorian Liberalism was about the workers being passively misled by the bosses. However, the educated, in particular, when judged by the stereotyped historical judgements of the English liberal tradition, were wrong—wrong about democracy, about Protection, about slavery possibly—though there were always many who were right. Right and wrong here are intended not as absolute, but only as relative to what have become the dominant

c

values of our political tradition; still, the strength of attachment to the Tory party shown by those possessing mental advantages at the very times when such an attachment was most imprudent, superfluous, or unattractive, may well be pondered over.* What there was acting for change among the rich—and their party preferences were of course far more evenly divided than today— came not from the advantages of education, but from the splendid panache of a political aristocracy, and from the social isolation of the usually badly educated commercial class. To do justice to the general electoral situation, it is necessary somehow to contemplate at once the existence, indeed the centrality, of force, power, co- ercion, defeat, in an almost military sense, between different groups, and the frequency with which the act of voting includes a claim to concern for some other group, which would by contem- porary standards have been considered alien or hostile.

Equally, the masses were not like the *tricoteuses*, vengefully bent on the overthrow of all ascendancy, yet the long term effect of their checkered and complicated behaviour did tend in that direction. Again it is necessary to be specific as to groups. At Preston in 1841, weavers voted Liberal by 3 to 1, but spinners only by 11 to 9. The railwaymen of York in 1852 were Tory by 2 to 1, but railwaymen elsewhere were Liberal. At Norwich in 1830, the textile employees voted Liberal in just about the same proportion as their employers, but the Norwich labourers were Tory. At Oldham in the 1850s, the popular party, and especially the industrial workers, tem- porarily fought under the Tory label against the Liberal mill- owners. It was not in any way the essence of the behaviour of the

* A special case which tends strongly against the above argument should be recorded here. This is Gladstone's defeat in the Oxford University election of 1865. Gladstone was not defeated by the resident electors, about 250 in num- ber, who voted for him by 155 to 89, including pairs on each side, but by new arrangements enabling the country clergy to vote by post. Many dons of course voted as Churchmen rather than as Liberals, Dr Pusey and Dr Routh for instance supporting Gladstone to the last. Yet even so a large majority of Oxford dons voted against a strong orthodox Conservative candidate in 1865. Sources: Noble, *Parliamentary Reformers' Manual* (1883), p. 30; J. Campbell, in *Oxford Magazine*, 9 November 1961; T. E. Kebbel, *Lord Beaconsfield and other Tory Memories* (1907), p. 305.

Similarly, we are told that in 1874 the masters at Harrow were 'Liberals almost to a man' (Lord Frederic Hamilton, *Here, There, and Everywhere*, 1921, p. 114) though G. W. E. Russell wrote of the Harrow boys in the more auspicious year of 1868, 'I remember only four, beside myself, who wore Liberal colours,' out of a school population of 500 (*Sketches and Snapshots*, p. 43). There is no real discrepancy here, because one would not expect dons and masters to behave in the same way as relatively well-educated people in the ordinary towns analysed below. Of more general relevance is the fact that even in 1906 all nine university seats remained Conservative.

masses to be hostile to those above them, merely the commonest form of it; and which groups among them did act like this, can only be ascertained, and not deduced.

6

It is now necessary to put into brief and condensed form the essentials of the relations between occupation and party preference. To do this, it is necessary to omit from the start certain elections, a substantial minority, where the fight was not on party grounds, or sociologically interesting motives were not given a clear turn. Where a Jewish candidate was standing (Maidstone 1841), where each village voted almost *en bloc* (Lincolnshire 1823), or where politics polarized about support or opposition to a landlord (Peterborough 1852), the voting patterns are of irreducibly particular interest. What can be generalized are the patterns in the majority of elections which were fought on party lines, which were and can be discussed in terms of class relations, and which had ideological overtones. (Party feeling is susceptible of numerical proof, e.g. at Yarmouth in 1830, only 12 votes out of 3,300 were not on a straight party ticket.) The following simplification of the empirical data was made by simple appraisal, rather than by statistical process, owing to the lack of any true principle for weighting and correlating different elections.

Ratio of Liberal to Tory votes

	Market town	Provincial metropolis	Industrial town
Gentlemen	1 : 1	1 : 1 to 1 : 2	2 : 3
Business	3 : 2	1 : 1 to 1 : 2	2 : 1 to 1 : 1
Professions	2 : 3	1 : 2	1 : 2
Shopkeepers	1 : 1 to 2 : 1	1 : 1 to 2 : 1	1 : 1 to 2 : 1
Craftsmen	1 : 1 to 2 : 1	1 : 1 to 2 : 1	1 : 1 to 2 : 1
Labourers	2 : 3	2 : 3	1 : 1

These ratios are all rather low. The few really high ones recorded come from places where one particular craft was extremely concentrated, though not necessarily working in factories, and from the landed gentry in county constituencies. In the first category, the shoemakers of Northampton were for Reform in 1831 by about 5 to 1, being opposed by most of the gentlemen, lawyers, and publicans; in Norwich in 1830, the textile workers were for Reform by 2½ to 1, while the cordwainers were so only by 5 to 3; the

Leicester framework knitters voted Liberal by 4 to 1; the voting for Orator Hunt at Preston in 1830 was highest—6 to 1—among the most numerous group, the weavers, and much less among similar but smaller skilled groups like mechanics or spinners, who supported Hunt by only 2 to 1. (The same feature persisted at Preston in 1841.) The distinguishing feature in these cases is surely not any difference in the relations of production from those of the isolated, normally only mildly radical, craftsmen, but simply the change in consciousness produced by a literally physical solidarity. At the other end of the scale, the country gentlemen were Tory* by perhaps about 4 to 1, except in the great volte-face of 1830–2. Hence the curious feature of the apparent classlessness in voting at the top of the borough electorate may in fact result from deadlock between two counteracting patterns of conflict over authority, and not from absence of conflict at all; the two patterns being conflict for authority within the town, and conflict between the town hierarchy and the external authority of the landed interest. The second conflict, if perhaps more factitious, was more general and more overt. On the occasions when a Radical candidate did challenge the position of rank within a town, as with Orator Hunt at Preston, or the Chartists at Nottingham or Halifax, the upper crust closed its ranks with almost perfect discipline, and classlessness melted away overnight. But the existence of an external upper class outside the borough electorate, in conflict with the town community as a whole over political authority, is necessary, not to account for the existence of two parties within the town—the tendency of consensus to generate coalitions of fragmentary opposed interests is enough for that—but to explain why the consensual party should generally be Liberal.

7

The next point is to relate the typical voting pattern given above, to the social structure. In the first place, the political society, at least as enfranchised in the three types of constituency chiefly analysed, was pre-industrial. ('In industrial societies, nearly one out of every two citizens of such societies earns his living in industrial enterprises of production.'†) No group was linked to

* The best statistical evidence for their Toryism is the table on the Cambridge-shire election of 1868 in H. J. Hanham, *Elections and Party Management* (1959), p. 26.
† Dahrendorf, *Class and Class Conflict in Industrial Society* (1959), p. 142.

another by the cash nexus, or by the relations arising from production, except in a tenuous and indefinite way. (The labourers are no doubt a probable exception.) The characteristic relation was that of vendor and customer, not employer and employee. Conflict might emerge instantaneously, over a particular transaction, or reflectively, over jealousy of inequality, but not automatically and constantly, through the antagonism of differing groups competing for the rewards of the general flow of production in which they participated. There was no economic basis for conflict between regularly defined and constantly opposed groups, in the sense that if these ones were to have more, those must have correspondingly less. And, as has been shown, particular economic pressure groups were unusual. Therefore, by elimination, the basis of electoral conflict lay in the political order.

This is not to say that denominationalism, or beliefs about change, or some other immaterial entity, was the *primum mobile*. Electoral conflict was in fact primarily between groups, the hard cores of which were defined and constituted by economic categories, and which, though not in economic conflict except marginally (e.g. fiscally), developed from their economic dissimilarities, separate political consciousnesses and wills to authority. The economic element serves only to constitute the personnel involved on each side; the difference of interest, and the object of the struggle, are political, not economic.

The essential division was between distributed property (mainly urban) and concentrated property (mainly rural), between capitalist agriculture and distributist urban petty production and exchange, between an urban 'free peasantry' and the great capitalists who ruled the only real Marxian proletariat that England had, the labourers in husbandry. There were all shades and degrees of exceptions, undeniably: the cotton industry on the one hand and peasant districts like Cornwall or parts of the Fens on the other, for instance; but here it is only towns in general and the countryside in general that are intended. Hence the perennial schizophrenia of the radical ethic, hovering between two sets of unstated assumptions about social structure, seething at inequality yet cherishing property and individual achievement, and hence too the stability of the preoccupations which re-emerged in rank and file liberalism. Their tone goes back in English history through the pamphlets of the 'freeholder interest' in eighteenth-century county elections, to the plain speakers of the Commonwealth; and, among foreign analogies, from the contest of Luther with the Fuggers, to the populism of the prairies, the most expressive at least is Proudhon's quite untheoretical love of decent poverty as the cornerstone of justice.*

The *pièces justificatives* necessary to demonstrate what has been said about the relative concentration of ownership and units of production in agriculture and industry, and the implications as to the general occupational and electoral structure of the country, are omitted here, and the curious are referred to the bibliography for the scant information available. The relevant statistics are few, intricate, and defective, and rather than make a travesty of analysing the rather mysterious Victorian social structure *en passant*, what have been set forth here are really heads of proposals for imaginative reconstruction of a political system.

8

The *Annual Register* for 30 January 1869 describes the funeral of Ernest Jones, the Chartist and semi-Marxist agitator, as

one of the largest public funerals which has been seen in Manchester for some years. At the head of the procession were the executive of the United Liberal Party, and the executive of the Reform League. Several thousand persons joined the procession. The streets were lined with dense crowds. Following in some of the 50 carriages were the Mayor of Manchester; Sir Elkanah and Benjamin Armitage: Jacob Bright, M.P.: Beales, Odger, Howell: T. B. Potter, M.P. The pallbearers were Edward Hooson, Jacob Bright, Elijah Dixon, Edmond Beales, Ald. Heywood, T. B. Potter, Sir E. Armitage, F. Taylor, James Crossley, Rev. H. M. Steinthal, Mr H. Rawson, and Mr Thomasson.

These names, renowned in their day, included several millowners, including two or three very wealthy ones; one or two newspaper editors; the London radical orators; the Manchester civic élite; and the leaders of the working class in the co-operative, trade union and reform movements. And Ernest Jones was a close correspondent of Karl Marx ('mein lieber Jones'); in many ways,

---

* Even 'anti-Utopian' extreme radicals glowed at the thought of a property-owning democracy. See the speech by Ernest Jones, a radical closely connected with Karl Marx, reported in the *Birmingham Daily Post*, 27 November 1867: 'England's wealthiest Ballarat is England. Our true goldfields are golden fields of wheat. Back to the land. It is your only safeguard against the assaults of capital. Talk of confiscating wealth. I propose to give it a legion of additional defenders. It is a national regenerator. Give us a million peasant farmers.'

for a long time, himself a Communist; and the most able, spirited, and class conscious of the Chartist survivors—a kind of English Lassalle, in fact. And yet here he is, buried with kindness; the little town had seldom seen a costlier funeral. This kind of political behaviour—which is only *in parvo* what one finds throughout the Liberal movement—has sometimes understandably promoted the view that political man was different in 1869, more silly, more crafty, or more charitable, according to one's point of view.

It is the same with the voting studies carried out here. When one has finally reached typical ratios of preference for the chief groups, one finds they do not very obviously manifest any sociological meaning, written as it were on the face of the sun for all to see. The question is therefore to find what kind of ideas of class would fit the known facts, in the first place; and in the second place, afford some explanatory insight into why the facts are as they are.

In the first place, there is little correlation (though what there is, is more positive than negative) between voting and class in the colloquial sense, that is, class as stratum, the statistical category of people united by having certain objective criteria of stratification, not conscious of itself as such and not doing anything as such. In this sense, there is a weak, but general and detectable, form of class conflict, meaning conflict between objectively defined strata, between 'rich' and 'poor'. The trouble with the use of 'class' in this sense is that it defines what is at best a weak potentiality, a statistical probability, corresponding to nothing anyone ever felt, and that it leaves what actually did happen, the people who actually did vote together, as naked of conceptual mantle as before. Class as stratum then, class in the colloquial sense, cannot really be used to describe voting patterns, or to explain them.

Secondly, there is Marxian class, engaged in conscious struggle as such, and generated by the relations involved in production. 'Individuals form a class only in so far as they are engaged in a common struggle against another class.'* This deeply interesting definition cannot however be applied in an unsophisticated Marxist way to the matter in hand, on two grounds. In the first place, as already argued, the political situation of electors did not in general involve capitalism, factory production, a propertyless proletariat, or personal relations arising from the conditions of production. It was exactly the lack of any such relations which produced radicalism. In the second place, in the exceptional cases

---

* Marx, cited in Dahrendorf, *op. cit.* p. 134.

of industrial situations to which the Marxian formula might be analytically fitting, it is generally factually incorrect. This is, unity between masters and men was usually greatest in these areas; that when a state of acute class difference arose, it could dissolve into warm class collaboration again in a short time, as at Oldham in 1852 and 1865; and that when masters and men were on different sides, the masters were usually still to the left of other, more 'disinterested' sections of the rich and influential. Only in 1868, in the voting of some groups of railwaymen and labourers, does the beginning of a new, truly 'industrial' pattern begin to appear. Nor was collaboration* simply on the terms of the boss; the largest manufacturer in Halifax, Crossley, voted for the Chartist candidate, Ernest Jones, in the Halifax election of 1847. The Marxian idea of class, as deriving from the relations of capital and labour, is interesting in proportion as it shows what the situation was not like and what did not happen. It describes and interprets nothing.

Dahrendorf differs from Marx, not as regards the active, purposive, nature of class and class conflict, but over the need to refer to the character of the economic society to define class. 'Classes are neither primarily nor at all economic groupings.'† In fact, on his model, the conflicts of bourgeoisies and aristocracies were the great fundamental type of class conflict, not merely the overture to the real thing: while the conflict of capital and labour is relatively local, and the tendency to interpret class conflict in these terms, almost a culture trait.

Drawing in part on his terms and definitions, with modifications for difference of subject, I would say that the voting patterns can be satisfactorily interpreted in terms of class and class conflict, and perhaps have to be. Political conflict at rank and file level was mainly between classes (the exceptions enumerated above not being sufficient to affect the general point). *These classes were not strata of rich and poor as in the colloquial sense of class, nor capital and labour as in the simplest Marxian sense of class.* These classes did, however, resemble Marxian classes, in that they were operational collectivities, acting at national level to achieve or prevent general changes in the structure of the political order (including the Church), and in lesser degree, to change the kind of person in

---

* Another curiosity was the case of the old Owenite, Weston, who was on the inner committee of the First International in 1864, although he was a manufacturer (of handrails).
† Dahrendorf, *op. cit.* p. 139.

authority; and that they acted thus, not blindly or from their appetitive natures, but because they were conscious of what they wanted to do, because they saw their action as part of a natural class effort without which it would have been meaningless, and because they, on both sides, used a socially agreed interpretation of the political structure and its economic basis. (The high *visible* intelligibility of a society of market towns and stately homes must be borne in mind—the social system was, so to say, expounded in the streets. Bath and Brighton both caught radicalism of an especially plebeian kind.) Moreover, despite the natural scatter of opinions, an appreciable section of each class wanted total structural change in the political order on the one hand, total adherence to the ancient constitution, a term of the widest import, on the other. The totality of persons engaged in achieving, abetting, or frustrating this political transformation forms an *operational* collectivity; it corresponds to parts of various social strata, themselves not operational units; and it is not the mere numerical aggregate of small primary groups, since the reasons for which people voted in groups locally cannot be understood at any level below their understanding of the structure of the national society, and their sense of belonging without local mediation to a collectivity acting directly in relation to that structure. This totality, then, though it might be said pedantically that its name was an open question, vivid though the experience of it was, is surely the one to which the name of class can fitly be attached. It is a collectivity operating in politics at a general level, non-economic in that it aims at authority in the political order, only partly economic as regards how its personnel are constituted, and it is not a political party proper. Which term of discourse is so fit to label this great white whale as class, especially as we have seen that class lacks other adequate homes?

This would accord very well with the presence of an acute class sense in mid-Victorian political consciousness (i.e. *la vision dichotomique* of social structure was practically a matter of folk culture in areas that had never heard a loom creak), co-existing with relatively or even entirely 'classless' patterns of voting even in quite free and pure elections. This would also fit well the fact that the economic upper stratum in towns did not vote like one, but did vote like a middle group in a stratification by authority, in which the external aristocracy were, and behaved like, the top group.

Two points of refinement are necessary. First, one must distinguish between the nature of a struggle between classes for authority, and the struggle, which may be on a generous scale, between competing élites of 'Ins' and 'Outs' for office or for points of polity, within an unquestioned framework of aristocratic society. The two are quite different; but confusion arises because the 'Ins' and 'Outs' of the aristocratic élites were superimposed on the class struggle. The classes were not interested in the personal enjoyment or exercise of power, but in the relative distribution of authority between themselves. Secondly, while it is necessary to reject outright, at least at the level of definition, the idea that classes were economically constituted groups acting for economic motives to effect change in the economic order, one must recede from dramatic negation at the level of description, and admit that political class had an economic flavouring. What is relevant is that the belief that it was natural for the rich and poor to be on opposite sides, for economic reasons, was far more widespread than was such behaviour in real life. There was a kind of sixth sense that the distribution of property was a function of the distribution of political power, even when all explicit tradition of how society worked ignored or denied this. Hence, in the case of the Tory majority group among the landowners and the radical majority group among the *menu peuple*, political behaviour was influenced by a general agreement as to where their economic interest lay, by the tendency of politicians to address them as economically defined and engaged groups, and by their own explanation of their behaviour in terms of an economically constituted group. On the other hand, all this makes the behaviour of the minority groups in each stratum harder to explain. The obvious conclusion is that the knowing, mysterious sideways glance that people used to suggest the implications of politics for the economic order, did not stop people doing what they wanted to do and would have done anyway, on the basis of social relations and the stratification of political authority alone.

9

To the view set forth above of the centrality of class, in a certain sophisticated sense, in rank and file political orientation, may be opposed three limiting or modifying propositions. The first, a necessary and acceptable limitation, is that the ordinary political activity of the period belongs to an autonomous political culture and has still to be explained as such. Class was diluted by party,

by events, by personality. It always needed incarnation in something of lesser generality which itself cannot be reduced to class
terms. Class was largely irrelevant to the life of Parliament, the
policy and preoccupations of the executive, or face to face politics
in general. The real question of importance here is how class
conflict could be retained for so long, endemic and in equilibrium,
in the electoral system, with so little impingement on policy, or on
the type of person in authority; the diversionary value of the electoral system, in focusing and resolving (if only by continued
adjustments till the next election) structural conflicts at a safe
distance from the world of political institutions and political culture, is suggested by this.

Secondly, it may be suggested that the word class as used here is
not so much erroneous as tautologous, the conception intended
being already well expressed by the more familiar idea of party.
This is not so. Both class and party are indeed operational units,
united by consciousness of themselves as such, rather than by
organization; and of maximum comprehensiveness. There similar-
ity ends and difference begins. Class is a homogeneous totality of
those whose main aim is structural change in the political society;
party is a heterogeneous alliance of people concerned to effect their
own aims through the party. Party might in fact be made up of a
core of 'class' and a fringe of 'interest groups' like the Catholic
vote or the drink or West India interests; it might conceivably, as
in Labour fundamentalism, be coterminous with class. But in fact
the dissonance between party and class was much greater than one
of fringes, for considerable sections in each party, entirely sound
from a party point of view, were opposed to or had no interest in
those ideas of political structure which animated the class-conscious
sections within each party. This is especially true of the Whig
leadership, of Disraeli, and of the Tory–Chartist working-class
vote. Party and class are ideas of like order, but they are not of one
nature.

Thirdly, there is the nominalist reproach against class, that
political orientation is real enough for individuals and for small
primary groups, but that classes, on the other hand, are just a
mental convenience existing for the purposes of generalization and
classification. This answers itself, for membership of an objectively
existent class was in general integral to, and antecedently necessary
for, individual political orientation. The existence of individual
opinion, and the objective reality of the entity 'class' engendered

by and yet also causing that opinion, stand or fall together. As for
the 'small primary groups', those Panzer battalions of the new
sociological approach, it is hard to think that they are the bricks of
which the building is built. As far as one can tell, a Baptist shoemaker would probably be as close in political opinion to a Congregationalist tailor unrelated to him living in another town, as to
a cousin of the same denomination and trade living in the same
town. It follows consequentially that membership of a class entails
membership of local groups, on the whole; but membership of a
local group does not entail class membership. There is also monu-
mental evidence, in the form of all political utterance from por-
tentous speeches to cartoons and ballads, that people do typically
see themselves as acting in a context of great generality (and,
conversely, find it much harder to visualize their role in a situation
'they know from their own experience', like municipal elections).

10

Careful investigation of voting habits shows how well founded are
many of the objections made against the idea of class (and especially
against the idea that it is the raw material with which politicians
have to work) by the sceptics and men of good will who have found
it a monotonous simplification of the richness of human situations.
One discovers a great flexibility of pattern and variety of data, and
a wide penumbra of sleepy backwaters with a political life in which
nothing is happening. Often it would be difficult, looking at
analyses of the voting of each party in an election, to decide by any
sociological criterion which was which. Then again, even in clear-
cut party battles fought with more than overtones of class, classlessness in party preference was vastly greater than today. The practical
moral for the politician of the nineteenth century, had he concerned himself with analysing pollbooks, would have been that
there is almost no quarter in which votes may not be sought and
won, no interest so sharply hostile that it is not worth placating,
that in short the electoral situation is profoundly plastic and
responsive to political art.

On the other hand, political art cannot undo what is elemental;
it cannot make a majority of those enjoying authority, vote for its
diminution, nor a majority of those without it, habitually vote for
their continued exclusion. Reason and education, and other things,
produced Liberal landowners and Tory craftsmen in numbers:
but never a secure majority of either. Whether or not class is

irreducible, it was in fact not reduced. Almost regardless of circumstances, the majority of the poorer people would vote for different candidates from the majority of the richer people (even when both sides were liberal, the class split was obvious, as at Glasgow, Brighton, and Edinburgh). Class, not in the Marxian sense of economic class, nor in the colloquial sense of stratum, but class in the sense of a group contending over the structure of political authority, was the general ground of popular political orientation.

II

THE DISTRIBUTION OF CAPITAL
AT DEATH: CAMBRIDGESHIRE 1848–57

This study is based on an examination of the grants of probate and administration made for all wills and intestacies occurring in Cambridgeshire (including Ely) in 1848–57 inclusive. These are to be found in the records of the four relevant courts, the Bishop's Court, the Archidiaconal Court, the Peculiar Court of Thorney, and the Prerogative Court of Canterbury* which had overlapping jurisdictions in the county up till the secularization of probate at the end of 1857. As over 90 per cent of entries give the occupation, or, in the case of women, the marital status, of the deceased, together with an indication of the amount left, they form a useful source for several problems in social history. Previous studies of capital distribution, such as those based on the death duties, have shown the distribution among socially unlocated holders. By using the probate records, it is possible to draw a general picture of social stratification, of the sectional distribution of capital between agriculture, manufacture and exchange, and of the internal capital structure within specific occupations, as well as dealing with the well-worn subject of simple inequality. The main features that emerge are so pronounced in Cambridgeshire, that it is hard not to think that a similar structure of ownership, differing only in degree, existed over a long period in the agricultural counties and market towns of much of England.† Three more general problems are therefore discussed: the conditions under which a capital structure of this type was compatible with economic growth, the motivation of individual economic action within such a structure, and the relation between popular political orientation in the towns and the system of ownership.

The statistics which follow are uncomplicated, but on four points a certain tolerance must be asked for. First, the category of 'gentlemen', which must have been a disguise for many of its

---

* I am indebted to Miss Peek of the Cambridge University Archives, and to the staff of the National Probate Registry, Somerset House, for instruction and guidance.

† The 1851 census divides the population of Cambridgeshire into 58,722 persons living 'in towns' and 133,172 persons living 'in the country parts'.

members who should properly have been placed in an earthier category, is irremediably impure. Secondly, grants of probate and administration were made only for one-tenth of all deaths, and this chapter proceeds on the assumption, made *ex silentio*, that those nine-tenths who do not reach the records died leaving little more than the clothes they stood up in, where they were not wives or minors. This is plausible, but the impossibility of recovering knowledge of working practice in these matters among the poor prevents a more positive basis than argument *ex silentio*. Thirdly, the distribution of capital at death is in certain cases not a good guide to the true distribution of capital among the living, e.g. it is fairly clear that widows would have held their capital for much shorter periods (and spinsters perhaps for longer periods) than the average holder of capital, and this would introduce a distortion into any analysis based on deaths. Fourthly, the sums at which estates were sworn are not proper valuations. It was sworn that an estate was 'under £450' or 'under £600', and it is this maximum figure which is used as the basis for computation. These maxima were always at certain conventional sums: £200, £300, £450, £600, £800, £1,000 and never at intermediate figures, i.e. there was no attempt at close valuation. Nevertheless, if an estate turned out larger or smaller than at first thought, the probate was carefully resworn, even for quite small changes: the matter was a serious one.

The figures which follow relate simply to the records, no attempt having been made to make adjustments for discrepancies between records and realities. The kinds of error in individual cases and quantities which the above remarks allow for are not sufficient to affect truths of proportion or the general tendency and implications of a multitude of instances.

More remarkable than the concentration of wealth among a few is the apparent complete absence of any effects among nine-tenths of male deaths:

	Total deaths 1848–57	No. of persons leaving property
Male	20,686	1,630
Female	19,797	694
	40,483	2,324

As probate and administration were granted for sums as small as £5 (three months' subsistence for a labourer), it is probable that even when abatement is made for the wives and minors, whose ability to own property was legally restricted, among the deceased, most people at death left savings and property which were very low in relation to their annual income.

Even within the 5 per cent of deceased who had anything to leave there was extreme inequality of distribution. The 76 men and women leaving over £10,000, though only 2·6 per cent of those leaving property and 0·2 per cent of all deaths, left almost 50 per cent of the wealth. The top 1 per cent of persons dying (400 persons, about 17 per cent of those leaving property) left £3,309,000 out of £4,415,000, i.e. about 75 per cent.

Women left about 17 per cent of all capital, distributed as follows:

	No. of persons	Total amount (£)
Wives	66	21,450
Spinsters	235	266,490
Widows	393	429,980
	694	717,920

This sum, left by only 3½ per cent of female deceased, was nevertheless larger than the amount left by all males engaged in agriculture, in this predominantly rural county.

Among the men, the general inequality of distribution by persons corresponded to an unequal division between various sectors of economic activity:

	No. of persons	Amount left (£)
A. Gentlemen, clergy, academics	291	2,326,000
B. All other males	1,339	1,371,000
C. All males with specific occupations, less farmers and those in (A) above	780	553,000
Total, all males	1,630	3,697,000

A more detailed table shows how little capital was needed for distribution, production, exchange, agriculture, and the small savings of employees, compared with the great quantity of wealth belonging to the genteel, which was not assigned to any specific economic role or function:

	No.	Total (£)	Median (£)
Gentlemen	242	1,655,000	1,500
Clergymen	39	413,000	2,000
Heads of Houses	6	203,000	22,000
Professors	4	55,000	15,000

	No.	Total (£)	Median (£)
Professions	72	118,000	450
Business	97	174,000	800
Farmers	359	663,000	1,000
Yeomen	151	39,000	100
Publicans	48	15,000	200
Shopkeepers	128	129,000	300
Craftsmen	178	42,000	100
Labourers	53	6,000	50
Mariners	8	9,000	375
Servants	45	21,000	200
Unstated	200	155,000	300
	1,630	3,697,000	

The only considerable body of highly capitalized producers was in agriculture. There were two nuclei in farming communities, grouped about £200 and about £4,000 respectively. The former were in much the same position as the small urban producers. Capital was a by-product of income, a consequence of the need for a small reserve and for ownership of some essentials. For the large farmer, his capital was the cause of his income. (This agrarian capitalism, be it noted, quite outmatched in wealth and numbers its urban counterpart—builders, brewers, millers, and maltsters.) The distribution of wealth among farmers, according to the conventional fixed points at which estates were estimated, was as follows:

Amount of estate	No. of persons	Total value (£)
£20 or under	26	460
£50	21	1,050
£100	36	3,600
£200	55	11,000
£300	25	7,500
£450	32	14,400
£600	18	10,800
£800	27	21,600
£1,000	18	18,000
£1,500	56	84,000
£2,000–£9,000	102	393,000
£10,000 and over	5	58,000
	359	663,000

It is not clear whether the term 'yeoman' has any specific meaning, or whether, if it has, it refers to status, to being a freeholder, or to being a small cultivator of any kind above the rank of labourer. The latter seems most probable. If the structure of the yeomanry

D

is laid alongside that of the farmers, the economic chasm between
petite culture and capitalist high farming is still clearer:

Amount of estate	No. of yeomen	Total value (£)
£20 and under	42	655
£50	24	1,200
£100	28	2,800
£200	18	3,600
£300	9	2,700
£450	9	4,050
£600	4	2,400
£800	6	4,800
£1,000	2	2,000
£1,500	7	10,500
£2,000 and over	2	4,000
	151	38,705

Disregarding marginal groups like labourers, servants, and
publicans, one finds a more egalitarian situation among shopkeepers and skilled workers and craftsmen. Apart from a group of
very substantial shopkeepers—such as booksellers, chemists,
drapers and wine merchants—the body of these people, such as
shoemakers, carpenters, grocers, butchers, bakers, tailors, left
effects amounting to about one to three years' income. (A craftsman's wage was about £50, taking one trade with another.) For
the craftsmen who were employees, not small masters, such a level
of savings in relation to income would be quite high by present-
day standards. But it must be remembered that an unknown number of craftsmen left practically nothing, and hence are not
recorded. The big shops apart, the shopkeepers were not on the
whole much better off than the skilled workers:

	Shopkeepers	Skilled workers
£20 and under	2	28
£50	13	25
£100	21	28
£200	23	30
£300	12	13
£450	10	9
£600–£800	11	5
		[£800–£1,000]
£1,000–£1,500	14	3
		[£1,500–£3,000]
£2,000–£8,000	20	4

The term 'gentlemen' is a net that catches many fish. But the
two most numerous strata, those leaving over £10,000, who were

landowning families like the Adeanes or Huddlestons, and those in the £2,000–£5,000 stratum, can reasonably be accepted as being generally free from 'trade' or from being merely pushing. The widows, like the shopkeepers and farmers, fall into two clusters, the widows of ordinary people, and the widows of gentlemen and rich farmers:

	Gentlemen	Widows
£50 and under	12	71
£100	14	74
£200	17	54
£300	13	33
£450	17	29
£600	15	22
£800	11	18
£1,000	9 [£1,000 and	
£1,500	20	over]: 90
£2,000–£5,000	54	
£5,001–£9,999	19	
£10,000–£49,000	33	
£50,000 and over	8	
	242	391

Where in all this are the middle class? for by tradition they should be reasonably conspicuous in an ordinary English county in 1850. It is not hard so much to find them, as to think them important. There is a clear lower middle class of craftsmen and shopkeepers, a manual and retailing middle class, fairly numerous, poor and homogeneous. There are the lower levels of the gentry, people who could live off their capital invested in the funds, and the block of rich farmers. But the kind of middle class, to which a history-making role has been assigned, was not thought of as rudely demotic, or merely genteel, or specifically rural. What was in mind was business and the professions. In Cambridgeshire, at least, these people were not numerically or economically dominant. Between them, they amounted to 10 per cent of males leaving property, and they owned 8 per cent of property left by males. When listed in detail, they look still less like the dynamic behind the historical process:

Business	No.	Amount (£)
Builders	14	19,300
Coal dealers	4	5,100
Carriers	2	400
Merchants	10	35,900
Ironfounders	2	800

Business	No.	Amount (£)
Coachmakers	2	300
Seedsmen	3	7,100
Upholsterer	1	16,000
Banker	1	4,000
Woolstapler	1	18,000
Millers	24	26,870
Coachbroker	1	1,000
Shipowner	1	200
Horse trainers	4	16,320
Brewers	11	7,050
Boatbuilders	2	500
Jobbers	9	5,450
Maltsters	5	9,600
	97	173,890

Professions, etc.	No.	Amount (£)
Bankers' Agent	1	450
Registrars	2	1,050
Dissenting Ministers	7	3,250
Clerks	5	750
Fellows	4	11,500
Gaol official	1	200
Tax collectors	2	550
Toll collectors	2	200
Curator, Botanic Gardens	1	4,000
Auctioneers	3	8,500
Organists	2	2,000
Librarian	1	3,000
Surgeons	10	27,400
Parish clerks	2	250
Civil engineers	3	500
Vet.	1	1,500
Lawyers	7	39,500
Pensioners	2	300
Schoolmasters	6	2,370
Officers	8	9,350
Workhouse masters	2	400
	72	118,000

The capital structure drawn above was top-heavy; it concentrated capital away from those actively engaged in the normal processes of production and distribution towards those least likely to engage in local business. The actual figures given over-emphasize the situation, because they do not allow for the numbers of local businessmen calling themselves gentlemen, or for the participation of the gentry proper in agriculture. Nevertheless, much of the wealth of the county was relatively functionless in relation to the local economic situation, and had to be understood in terms of status and family endowment and provision. The position in Cambridgeshire in the 1850s would fit the hypothesis that the extreme concentration of wealth, not in the hands of entrepreneurs and captains of industry, but in the hands of widows, spinsters, rich farmers, clergymen, academics, squires and rentiers claiming gentility, created a permanent 'underconsumptionist' obstacle to economic growth under the English *ancien régime*. The causes which drew wealth out of the general flow, into the large savings of the genteel, were certain, perennial, and independent of individual initiative. The causes operating to draw the wealth of the rich back into circulation were occasional, variable and usually required positive action. These things being so, nothing would be more important in the historical economics of nineteenth-century England than to show the conversion of this type of capital structure, locally and usually an incubus, into an asset at national level, whether through the building of railways and canals, or through deficit-financed French wars acting rather like a public works programme. State activity, acting through the national debt, poor rates and taxes to bring underemployed wealth of this kind into play, was probably necessary at first to combine this type of capital structure with rapid economic growth.

It is important to notice that the concentration and social localization of capital did not take place for business reasons. Production and technique had nothing to do with it: it was a process taking place outside the daily economy, which was manned, on the whole, by independent small producers. The chief exceptions were among some of the farmers, shopkeepers and a few businesses like builders, where large property did correspond to large units of economic activity. But broadly, the kind of capitalism drawn above was not connected with a sense of economic role or vocation, was not concerned with entrepreneurship or production, which was carried on by different strata, and neither caused, nor was caused by, a business ethic. Indeed, so far as the owners of capital had a coherent social ethic, they repudiated all these things, and especially 'trade'. Those who carried on the normal economic life of Cambridgeshire needed singularly little of its total capital to do so; those who had most of the wealth of the county required as a mark of caste at least an outward non-participation in economic activity.

The extreme inequality of this society is better represented by a withdrawal of wealth to one side, away from daily life, rather than its imposition from above over daily life. In this way, a high degree of inequality had some curiously egalitarian consequences for the social ethic and political orientation of the ordinary person. For the productive situation especially in the towns, but also among the small farmers and yeomen, remained egalitarian, and was unaffected by inequality of ownership. The general experience almost conformed to 'the American dream'. With hard work and thrift, any yeoman, shopkeeper, carpenter or shoemaker might reach affluence as it was understood by the people he knew. A labour theory of value was quite appropriate to such a situation, as was a morality of sturdy independence, and a sense of the fitness of political democracy. The milieu of the townsman who was just rising, doubtless by merit, from poverty into small property, was self-explanatory without reference to the inequalities in the wider national life, however great these were objectively; for to these real and great inequalities, there was no corresponding experience of economic domination or conflict in daily urban life. Hence the puzzling features of Victorian popular radicalism (strong, incidentally, in Cambridge), with its ambivalence towards wealthy aristocrats and its preference for political over economic aims. The latter has generally been considered either irrational, or a product of insidious upper-class pressure. But the picture of social structure sketched above argues strongly against this. Victorian society achieved very great inequality at the top without affecting the fraternity, liberty and equality of the crucial stratum of the town population—the craftsmen, retailers, publicans and skilled employees and small masters. This was because the inequality lay almost entirely in the realm of functionally superfluous capital, while productive capital remained comparatively evenly distributed. In such circumstances, politics were centred on conflicts over authority in the town, in Parliament and in the Church, between two milieus not normally in economic conflict, but too far apart in daily life not to react to each other in a xenophobic way.

III

THE POLITICAL FEELINGS OF
THE PEOPLE

In conclusion here is a psychological theory about the strange behaviour of 'the people' in modern English history. It starts from what is universally admitted in individual cases, that one person's needs may be chiefly material (money, housing, safety at work) and another's non-material (sociability, excitement, emotional satisfaction). Both needs are equally real and important and central to the action of those who have them. Can this simple individual distinction be generalized into a distinction of political psychology valid for large groups? In two cases at least, there are contrasting types of social situation inclusive enough to create a general psychological outlook among those they affect, irrespective of their 'personal character', which is submerged in public matters by their public, occupational function.

The social distinction which splits 'the people' broadly into two is between those who are institutionalized and given society by their work (mines, docks, large factories with *male* workers, labourers in Norfolk-type agriculture) and those whose work creates for them only an exiguous system of personal relations (petty producers, Cornish-type farmers,* retailers, tramping artisans, skilled craftsmen, small dealers). Nothing keeps people apart like small property.

* The contrast between the strength of Labour in rural Norfolk, and of the Liberal party in rural Cornwall, can be plausibly explained in terms of the local agrarian structure: it corresponds to the division between corn and grass, large farms and small farms, capitalist and peasant types of agriculture. See Hirsch, 'Size of Farm Holdings', *Farm Economist*, IX (1958), 87, for a map showing the strong east–west division in land ownership patterns. For Cornwall, see Daniell, *Cornwall* (1906), pp. 160–1, and Lawry, *J. Roy. Agric. Soc.* (1892). The average size of holdings in 1903 was:

All England	66·1 acres
Wales	46·6 acres
Cornwall	44·8 acres

9,700 holdings out of 13,500 in Cornwall in 1903 were between 1 and 50 acres. It was a peasant society. Even in 1954 there were still no farms over 1,000 acres in the county, and in 1965 some 53 per cent of the 12,011 holdings were classified as 'part-time holdings'.

For the first group, their work carries with it membership of an essentially political, highly structured, situation, on the model of a school. Also their material interests are quite clear cut, and conflict over them follows the same lines of division as conflict about authority in the institutional situation. Because the emotional interest available for politics is fixed and in part absorbed for these people at local level, the carry-over from them into national politics consists of strong 'rationalist' demands (Taff Vale, Beveridge) for practical objects conceived in material terms, accompanied by weakly supported 'ideological' demands (clause 4), drastic in formulation, but with no weight of feeling or intention behind them.

For the second group, the individualists (whether employers, self-employed, or employees in a small enterprise), the situation is rather the reverse. Their material situation gives no clear lead. Their job does not array them immediately in conflict of authority with a superior. Their economic hopes are miscellaneous and shifting. Voluntary arrangements may suit them better than the Welfare State. General and collective betterment, they rightly fear, may cost them money. Yet, combined with antagonism to disturbance in their personal milieu, was a need to express the feelings naturally arising in the small man from contemplating the successful and the holders of power. Decent poverty of this type had very deep frustrations, but its social base precluded any economic programme, except economy. How was an outlet to be found for the political side of such people? Not in local voluntary associations, which, whether religious, prudential, or convivial, were combinations based on 'niceness' and were ill-suited to express sterner feelings. (Some of the apparent authoritarianism of the small town Radical —e.g. as to penal views or hatred of Rome—may be explained in this way. They were not inherently more aggressive than other people, but their position forced them into an unnatural 'niceness' in so many relations of life, e.g. to customers, that their patience broke more quickly than others, when it found a socially approved object to hate.) The only way for them to assert that they were as good as the holders of authority and of the means of enjoyment, was through national politics, and in national politics the really interesting thing would be the transfer of power from 'them' to 'us', and generally any symbolic reform which commuted the individual helplessness of the Radical voter into a sense of power over his betters. This demand reached national politics more fiercely because it was unabsorbed by being filtered through, and partly used in, a local situation.* This is what Liberalism was for, so far as the people were concerned, to enable them to have nationally, the satisfaction daily and local life denied to them. It was therefore not necessary that Liberal measures should benefit them: so long as they vexed the mighty, this was a sufficient reason for enthusiasm. What Gladstone was offering was emotional subsistence level—the possibility of participation, antagonism, struggle, commitment, eventual victory, a sense of power and domination— to people normally entirely subject to circumstances and to other people. The permanent issue behind Midlothian and Reform and Home Rule was what kind of people should have power, in whose name, and in accordance with whose ideas. Gladstone offered the psychic satisfaction of ruling to the ruled—not ruling over themselves, but ruling and overruling the traditional holders of authority, or large parts of them, which was much more gratifying. Gladstone offered this for what it was, and the people accepted it for what it was—a question of self-determination and of the union of hearts: not of bread. Nobody deluded anybody.

Now we have here two quite different styles of popular politics. On the one hand 'industrial' situations produce sharp, but institutionally self-contained, industrial conflicts, which overflow into national politics via a strong organization-based leadership, making strong practical demands, and drastic-sounding but really unsupported ideological and structural demands, at the national level.† On the other hand, people in 'individualist' situations— although probably in the same economic and self-assessed stratum —generate the opposite pattern of political behaviour. Here the occasion is the national elections, there is no antecedent or intermediate stage of local or institutional conflict, leadership acts through opinion not organization, and the practical programme is as tinkering as the ideological demands are fierce. Both situations

---

* This pent-up resentment of environment, overflowing into national ideological politics because there is no local outlet, occurs in the Communist vote in France and Italy today, in entirely non-industrial areas. Perugia and Siena, cities of small craftsmen, are Communist, Milan and Turin are not. The Communist vote in certain backward rural departments in France, e.g. Corrèze, is rather similar to the peasant anti-clericalism of such Liberal strongholds as North Cornwall and the Isle of Ely.

† The miners are a good example of this dichotomy. At a local level, they are bitter: half of all strikes in Britain are in coal mining. At parliamentary level, the miners' members of Parliament, from 1900 to the rise of Gaitskell, have been silent pillars of the Labour Right.

may derive something from the personal shortcomings of political personnel, or from the intellectual cramps of a received body of 'objective knowledge', but the pattern is too deep to come from anything but a difference in the area of unsatisfied basic needs between the 'industrial' and the 'individualist' sections of the people.

The relative validity and good faith of each type of popular politics is a question of numbers. To offer, as a novelty, the delights of solidarity and collective action to miners and dockers, who have it every day of their lives, would obviously be as out of place as to proselytize the self-employed (such as the Sheffield 'little masters') on employers' liability, or to preach housing policies to people whose existence turned on inhabiting one particular corner-shop, pub, or low-cost home workshop. What then were the people—were they 'individualists' or 'proletarians', more like miners or more like cobblers?

The statistics will not run to an exact answer. There are no reliable factory statistics* before the later 1890s. The occupational census returns fail to distinguish masters from men with any success. Nevertheless, the majority of 'individualists' over 'proletarians', indicated by all the imperfect data at our disposal for the period before 1900, is quite a large one. It is larger if only adult males are reckoned on each side, for women and children probably formed half the factory population.† In the nineteenth century many advanced industries, which to the traveller's eye must have seemed classic cases of large-scale enterprises where a capitalist employer was linked to undifferentiated wage labour by a cash nexus, were still holding to the forms of social organization associated with petty producers in dispersed crafts linked to a market by mercantile entrepreneurs. The Birmingham trades were riddled with cases of workmen employing their own workmen. 'The manufacturer, even if he had a large factory, usually delegated much of his authority to overhands, and had little to do with the actual productive process. He was, in truth, a factor who had gathered his dependent craftsmen into his own establishment.' In some cotton trades the same man could be employer and employee:

* On the question of reliability, see 'Report of the Departmental Committee on Factory Statistics', *Parl. Papers*, 1895, XIX, 583.

† See *Parl. Papers*, 1871, LXII, 164: Returns of all persons employed coming under all Factories and Workshops Acts (no distinction being made between factories and workshops):

Total of all such persons for England	2,006,000
Total of whom males over 18	1,051,000

in the Sheffield crafts, the artisans were one week masters, next week employees, the next self-employed. Several coalfields also tried to organize mass production in the old small-scale groups through the butty system. In cotton, many mills were hired off, a floor or a loom at a time to very small operators, using their own labour. This obscure tendency of mass industry to go backwards to organization based on petty property and the creation of value by labour must have inhibited the growth of an employee mentality among workers. In Cornish mining, an important industry by world standards for most of the nineteenth century, the divergence from capitalist norms, through the practice by which groups of miners in effect rented mines and divided the profits, was even wider.*

The disparity in favour of pre-industrial life is further magnified when it is remembered that, for political purposes, what counted was the social structure, not in itself, but as distorted by an electoral régime which discounted concentrated industrial populations. (Before 1885 this electoral distortion was even greater.) If the psychological model used here is right, success in popular politics could only be had on Gladstonian lines, by recognizing that though the Radical voter did not want disturbance in his milieu, he found great vicarious excitement in identifying himself with an attack on authority, conducted as a public spectacle at national level. Gladstone created a national theatre for England as Verdi did for nineteenth-century Italy. To ask what the people hoped to get, say, from the election victory of 1880, is to ask the wrong question. What they primarily hoped to get was the election victory itself, as a visceral thrill, and as an assertion of their proper importance. Ulterior motives there were, but they were peripheral at popular level. The people went to the conflict like the Greeks went to the play. If the occupational aggregates are anything to go by, the political-psychological complexion and internal proportions of the population have changed little since 1850 (except by the enfranchisement of women). Change from small production to 'proletarian' types of production, and the decline in small property owners,† has been matched by a growth in white-collar employees.

* For Birmingham, see G. C. Allen, *The Industrial Development of Birmingham and the Black Country* (1929), p. 337; for Cornwall, see Warner, *A Tour through Cornwall* (1809), p. 229; and for a special case, see John Prest, *The Industrial Revolution in Coventry*.

† The number of publicans and beersellers in England and Wales fell from 113,000 in 1871 to 68,000 in 1964.

The psychic balance remains much the same.* The rural peasants have almost gone, but not the urban sources of the peasant mentality, or the general experience of domination in daily work, or the wide doubts as to the real advantage of politically won economic gains.

It is not too difficult to fit the change from Liberal to Labour, and the associated intensification of class attitudes, into this fairly stable occupational framework. It was not a question of changing distribution of occupations, so much as a remarkable difference in the ability of different groups to produce strong political institutions. With the stigma over the pubs, the chapels running to seed, and organizations like the National Union of Tobacconists hopelessly lightweight, great sections of the lower economic stratum were just not socially integrated enough to count. Also, an almost panic closing of the ranks against 'socialism' by the traditionally influential tended to make self-validating an initially false conception of what the change to Labour meant. The exaggeration of the change was due to special economic difficulties, interpreted by evolutionary pessimists imbued with a simple linear notion of historical change.

In fact, the Labour movement rose in an objective context not specially helpful to it, in a time of stable or declining relative employment in manual work in general and in manufacturing in particular. The situation was near enough to that of today (as pictured by revisionists) to suggest that the switch to a strongly 'proletarian' interpretation of the character of the manual workers was a subjective factor on both sides. Moreover, at that time the classical capitalism of the family firm was breaking up through the increasing differentiation of the labour force and the disintegration of the functions of the capitalist—processes often held to make for easing of conflict and 'post-capitalist' stability. Yet Labour *did* rise, and conflict *did* intensify. The reaction of the upper strata to practical demands for welfare through redistribution did differ sharply from their dealings with nineteenth-century demands for democratic participation. The twentieth-century conflict was more traumatic, and left less of a sense of flexible opportunism, of riding

---

* G. G. C. Routh, *Occupation and Pay in Great Britain, 1906–1960* (1965), states that while the proportion of manual workers fell from 81 to 70 per cent over 55 years, the proportion who were managers or proprietors has remained static over this period. Thus the figures hardly give a clear interpretative lead by themselves.

the storm, of fundamental ability to land on one's feet, than the change to a democratic franchise had produced in the politicians who carried it through.

But the issue raised by Labour was far less dangerous. The people seeing themselves as 'industrial masses'—rather forcedly—wanted what could well be given without general change in the political society. The people, typifying themselves as cobblers, had wanted to rule the Ascendancy of Church, land, and education, or at any rate to stop it ruling, even if it did this only by symbolic means (as with the disestablishment in 1868 of the Irish Church). Between Liberal and Labour the real revolutionary aim of English Jacobinism was lost sight of, and popular politics changed from being about power to being about bread. This change related directly to the *dominant conception* of social structure held by the people themselves and by political élites. This dominant conception changed in a way quite out of proportion to any changes in actual numbers in one group or another, and was much more over-drawn in favour of an 'industrial' interpretation of the people, than the Gladstonians had exaggerated their petty bourgeois and proprietary nature. One section of the people produced stable organization and striking leaders, the others were relatively void of institutional life, and people redrew their maps of the social structure accordingly, and incorrectly. The part was mistaken for the whole, and had in time to learn to speak for the whole and like the whole.

The method of change from Liberal to Labour was not by numbers, but, like the rise of Rome, due to weight of institutions. But the dropping of power as the central motive in popular politics was not just the replacement of an old idea by a new one, but corresponded very closely to the psychological needs created by the new supposedly dominant set of daily circumstances. There was a negative correlation between industrialization and revolu-tion, considered from the point of view of popular contumacy and the probability of real change in the seat of power, and the type of person occupying it. There was a positive correlation between industrialization and revolution so far as the use of political power to benefit the poor at the expense of the rich goes. The latter criterion has been too much in favour at the expense of the political criterion. Both are very important. Each corresponds to the political psychology engendered by an archetypal occupational situation. Working with welfare as criterion, the Gladstonian Liberals were a pusillanimous prelude to Labour. Working with power and the total structure of society as terms of reference, the Liberals were much more drastic revolutionaries than Labour. To prefer the criterion of welfare is not only to neglect the extraordinary and lasting nineteenth-century achievement in the deliberate total structural change of the political society, but to foist a modern *Realpolitik* of bread, on men who needed politics chiefly to supply the circuses of their lives.

IV

NOTES ON THE MEANING OF THE
OCCUPATIONAL CATEGORIES USED
IN ANALYSIS

A fairly standard definition and classification of the significant occupational categories was evolved in preparing these tables. This classification had necessarily to be somewhat personal and arbitrary: also, there are in any case irreducible difficulties involved in using occupational descriptions which are based ultimately on the pleasant process of self-assessment of status. (Other causes of ambiguity, such as corruption or the same person holding several jobs, are not dealt with here, since they do not relate to the text of the pollbook.) A careful explanation of the procedure followed in compiling the tables is therefore important.

The first rule was to stick to the descriptions given in the pollbook, wherever possible; where the pollbook described a man as a 'banker', to write him down as a banker, and not otherwise. In many cases this procedure was followed unflinchingly. Only those described as merchants and grocers were set down as such; and mere 'corn merchants' and 'shopkeepers' were spurned. But this policy of no alteration to the classification given in the pollbook could not be followed to its limits. For instance, 'butchers' in the following tables includes those described as 'pork butchers', and 'gentlemen' includes those listed only as esquires. A measure of conflation or adulteration of categories was as necessary in some cases, as it would have been unfortunate in others. Also, in some cases the nature of the question asked dictated a different approach. There was little interest in the possible differences in voting between different grades of railwaymen and policemen, but much in the question how far the personnel of a railway or of a police force voted as a corps. In these and similar cases, where it is the general tendency of an institution that is at stake, the various grades of personnel were conflated into one category. The officers of the different services were also grouped together for convenience.

The normal practice (not always followed in the earlier analyses, since it was only reached *ambulando*) was as follows: 'Gentlemen' in the tables corresponds to 'gentlemen' and 'esquires' in the pollbooks. 'Officers' in the tables means all kinds of officers. 'Bankers' means simply bankers. 'Surgeons' includes those stated to be 'physician' or 'M.D.'. 'Lawyers' includes barristers, solicitors, and attorneys. Tailors are simply tailors, and carpenters do not include joiners. Grocers are grocers, but butchers may include pork butchers. Labourers do not include labouring men like navvies or bargemen, but only those described as labourers. The category of farmers may sometimes include a few yeomen. 'Cordwainers' includes shoemakers, bootmakers, and cobblers, but not cloggers, who are stated separately. Brewers are only brewers, and not maltsters. Beersellers include the synonymous beerhouse and alehouse keepers; publicans include victuallers and innkeepers. 'Merchants' means only merchants unqualified by any specific prefix. Manufacturers, equally, are those set down as such by the pollbook, where no information is given as to what they manufacture.

'Engineers' and 'firemen' carry an awkward double meaning in this period: the reader is left to decide whether they were really railwaymen or not. Still more awkward is the word 'clerk'. This can mean an Anglican clergyman, or it can mean a man who works in an office. Only the context can decide: office workers do not live in country vicarages. Apparently the terms 'clerk' and 'clergyman' always refer to an Anglican, and the term 'minister' always to a Nonconformist. Certainly, the voting patterns which emerge from such working assumptions strongly confirm their correctness. Most county pollbooks do not state the occupations of voters, but it is easy to pick out the names prefixed by 'Rev.', and thus to show the voting of Anglican clergy in the county elections. A few Nonconformist ministers may perhaps creep in to swell the apparent Liberal vote among the Anglican clergy. If so, this would only emphasize further the Toryism of the Church of England which stands out sufficiently already in the tables below.

Over a wide range of crafts and manufactures it is not possible to distinguish between master and man, capitalist and employee, retailer and craftsman, factory worker and domestic worker. This simply has to be accepted, for it is much more than a simple defect of information. Its real meaning is that although there were considerable differences of situation and of economic and technical function among skilled craftsmen and small entrepreneurs and retailers, there was nevertheless a feeling that people engaged in making the same kind of thing were the same kind of people. Emulation came into it, but it was hardly emulation that stopped master shoemakers so calling themselves, just as much as wage-earning shoemakers discarded the term of journeyman. Emulation today does not make workers describe themselves as directors; and if in the nineteenth century the pattern of self-description implies that the social distance a shoemaker might move above and below the normal shoemaker was not important to them, then probably it was not objectively important either. The compilers of the Census found this problem insoluble, and a Dr Ogle defended their failure in an illuminating way:

It was suggested, as it had been suggested many times before, that the employers should be distinguished from the employed...He could assure Mr Booth that nobody was more anxious than those concerned in the census that, were it possible, such a distinction should be made, and special directions were given on the schedule that every worker should state whether he was master or man: but it was all in vain: workmen would not do anything of the kind. He believed that out of the 26 millions of people in England and Wales, there were not 1,000 who had returned themselves as journeymen anything. A man called himself a baker, whether he were a journeyman baker, or master baker, and so with other trades: it was impossible to distinguish them.*

These remarks apply to the pollbooks as much as to the Census. Only in Lancashire, and later in Yorkshire and Leicestershire, can one distinguish with confidence between employer and employed.

Most of the tables which follow analyse only some of the many occupations in each constituency. Necessity and reason alike justify this. Wherever an unusual feature occurred, such as the fullers in Exeter, the pinners in Gloucester, or the papermakers in Maidstone, it was included for analysis, though it was necessarily of little general significance. Secondly, some occupations, like publicans, pilots, sweeps, or turnkeys, were analysed to try and uncover the effect of some trade question, legislation, or institutional influence on voting. Thirdly, certain typical, widespread, fairly numerous occupations were chosen as 'indicators' of class feeling or its absence among a much wider body of men of whom they were considered to be fairly representative. To have analysed more constituencies completely might have enabled one to say more exactly just what contingencies each election turned on, but it would have been unlikely to uncover further abnormal or anomalous groups, and it would have added little to the data given below for a study of political orientation. The 'indicators' chosen—or

* *Journal of the Royal Statistical Society* (June 1886), p. 438.

E

rather, which chose themselves—were usually bankers, merchants, manufacturers, clergy, surgeons, lawyers, and officers for the upper crust; shoemakers, tailors, weavers, grocers, butchers, for the craftsmen and tradesmen; and labourers, shipwrights, and mariners, where these occurred.

Far the most gnomic term is 'gentleman'. They are numerous and ubiquitous: they are usually Tory, but not nearly so much so as the clergy and the professions, and they may sometimes be chiefly Liberal. The 'gentleman' of the borough pollbooks is clearly of a different and lower order from the landed gentleman of the counties. For one thing, the urban 'gentleman' may be a Dissenter. For another, he may be in business—he might even be a shopkeeper beneath his broadcloth. The urban 'gentleman' is defined by the view from below, not from above; he is a gin'lman, a gent, but not quite a toff. He is nearer to the counting house than to the playing fields of Eton, but he does not really belong anywhere. Because it is such a ragbag of a category, the term 'gentleman' is very useful to us in tracing opinion among the urban well-to-do in general.

In towns like Leicester and Preston, those specifically textile occupations which hardly occur elsewhere were tabulated, though some among so many had to be omitted. In all towns, any occupations, whether of employer or employed, which seemed to involve factory production, mechanization, or capitalist forms of production, were taken note of—with disappointingly thin results for anyone seeking to get a grip on the political consequences of the Industrial Revolution. (In passing, it must be remarked how little political weight the great metal making and using industries had outside Sheffield and the Black Country.) If the tables below fail to contain many 'modern' industrial people, this is partly because of the maldistribution of the existing pollbooks, but it is chiefly because such people were not there. Probably they did not exist: but if they did, they did not have the vote. The absence of industrial people is not due to choice of the wrong categories. The following tables have their defects, but the principles upon which they have been analysed do provide data necessary for a general view of political orientation in this period. Refusal to make rough generalizations, on the basis of the evidence gathered below, would involve magnifying the admitted snags and untidiness of the data, into a sense of the mystery of the things which is rather out of place in dealing with 'beer, brawls, and bribery'.

TABLES OF VOTING

A. OCCUPATIONS ANALYSED BY CONSTITUENCIES*

1. The voting of Roman Catholic priests, 1832–72†

Election	Leading Liberal	Leading Tory	Second Liberal	Second Tory
Beverley 1854	1	0	—	—
Brighton 1841	1	0	1	—
Bristol 1837	1	0	0	—
Bristol 1841	2	0	0	—
Bristol 1852	1	0	—	—
Cambridge 1859	1	0	1	0
Cambridge 1865	1	0	1	0
Cambridge 1868	1	0	1	0
Glasgow† 1832	1	—	1	—
Ipswich 1847	1	0	0	—
Ipswich 1857	1	0	0	0
Ipswich 1859	1	0	0	0
Ipswich 1865	0	1	0	1
Leicester 1847	1	0	1	0
Lindsey 1835	2	0	1	—
Liverpool 1835	4	0	4	0
Maidstone 1870	1	0	—	—
Northampton 1831	1	0	1	0
Oldham 1865	1	0	—	—
Reading 1837	1	0	1	—
Sandwich 1868	1	0	1	—
Shrewsbury 1847	1	0	1	—
Tamworth 1837	1	1	0	—

* The blank entries in this and the following tables may mean either that no third and fourth candidates were standing, or that, if they were, votes given for them were not tabulated by the present writer.
† In the Glasgow election of 1832, the Catholic bishop voted for the two successful Whig candidates.

2. The voting of organists, 1852–72

Election	Leading Liberal	Leading Tory	Second Liberal	Second Tory
Beverley 1859	0	2	—	1
Bristol 1852	0	3	—	—
Cambridge 1859	0	3	0	3
Cambridge 1863	0	3	—	—
Cambridge 1865	0	3	0	3
Cambridge 1866	0	2	—	—
Cambridge 1868	0	5	—	—
Ipswich 1852	1	1	0	0

The voting of organists, 1852–72 (cont.)

Election	Leading Liberal	Leading Tory	Second Liberal	Second Tory
Ipswich 1857	1	1	1	1
Ipswich 1859	0	1	0	1
Leicester 1859	0	1	1	—
Maidstone 1865	0	1	—	—
Oldham 1865	0	1	—	—
Rochester 1852	0	1	0	1
Rochester 1856	0	1	—	—
Rochester 1859	0	1	0	1
Rochester 1868	0	1	—	—
Shrewsbury 1868	0	1	0	—
York 1852	0	1	0	—

3. The voting of sextons, 1852–72

Election	Leading Liberal	Leading Tory	Second Liberal	Second Tory
Beverley 1854	1	0	—	—
Bristol 1852	0	6	—	—
Bury St Edmunds 1852	1	1	0	—
Cambridge 1857	0	1	0	1
Cambridge 1868	0	1	0	1
Ipswich 1857	0	1	0	1
Ipswich 1859	0	1	0	1
Ipswich 1865	0	1	0	1
Maidstone 1865	0	1	—	—
Maidstone 1870	0	1	—	—
Northampton 1852	0	2	0	—
Sandwich 1868	1	0	1	0
Shrewsbury 1868	0	1	0	—
Southampton 1852	0	1	0	1

4. The voting of labourers, 1830–72

Election	Leading Liberal	Leading Tory	Second Liberal	Second Tory
Abingdon 1830	0	1	—	—
Ashton 1841	13	10	—	—
Bedford 1841	56	46	—	46
Bedford 1857	17	23	—	—
Beverley 1840	25	37	—	—
Beverley 1854	30	24	—	—
Beverley 1859	53	36	—	25
Bolton 1835	1	1	0	—
Brighton 1841	29	16	19	—
Bristol 1832	142	191	125	—
Bristol 1837	108	140	—	112
Bristol 1841	87	104	—	97

The voting of labourers, 1830–72 (cont.)

Election	Leading Liberal	Leading Tory	Second Liberal	Second Tory
Bristol 1852	69	72	—	—
Bury St Edmunds 1852	1	1	—	0
Cambridge 1835	5	5	4	—
Cambridge 1840	6	11	—	—
Cambridge 1845	5	12	—	—
Cambridge 1857	3	8	3	7
Cambridge 1859	4	5	4	5
Cambridge 1863	3	3	—	—
Cambridge 1865	7	1	6	1
Cambridge 1866	5	7	—	—
Cambridge 1868	214	108	—	—
Dover 1837	36	36	—	26
Durham 1843	3	3	—	—
Hereford 1832	14	21	13	—
Hereford 1835	11	12	12	—
Ipswich 1852	22	7	21	5
Ipswich 1857	15	6	15	6
Ipswich 1859	23	11	8·	12
Ipswich 1868	186	160	—	—
Leicester 1847	17	30	17	—
Leicester 1859	17	41	28	—
Leicester 1861	11	62	4	—
Lewes 1835	24	26	4	—
Lewes 1837	14	17	—	—
Lincoln 1835	9	38	6	—
Lincoln 1841	11	42	10	40
Lincoln 1848	25	33	—	—
Liverpool 1835	89	60	76	54
Loughborough 1830	6	4	—	—
Maidstone 1841	15	55	—	50
Maidstone 1857	33	58	33	57
Maidstone 1865	65	82	—	—
Northampton 1852	14	44	9	—
Norwich 1830	10	23	7	21
Nottingham 1852	9	29	—	—
Reading 1841	3	1	3	1
Rochdale 1857	3	2	—	—
Rochester 1835	6	7	3	—
Rochester 1852	18	17	18	17
Rochester 1856	19	23	—	—
Rochester 1859	16	18	16	18
Rochester 1865	23	16	18	—
Rochester 1868	180	116	—	—
Sandwich 1852	2	21	—	—
Sandwich 1859	14	19	11	17
Sandwich 1868	119	102	128	—
Shrewsbury 1837	19	16	17	15
Shrewsbury 1868	131	147	85	—

The voting of labourers, 1830–72 (cont.)

Election	Leading Liberal	Leading Tory	Second Liberal	Second Tory
Shropshire 1831	44	88	30	64
Shropshire (North) 1832	45	54	29	—
Tamworth 1837	28	46	—	27
Tamworth 1841	27	47	—	23
Warrington 1847	10	17	—	—
York 1835	23	49	8	—
York 1852	33	43	21	—

In 41 of the above cases the leading Tory received more votes than the leading Liberal; in 20 cases the leading Liberal received more votes.

5. The voting of shoemakers, 1830–72: sample cases from 'normal' elections

Election	Leading Liberal	Leading Tory	Second Liberal	Second Tory
Ashton 1841	20	8	—	—
Bedford 1841	28	36	—	—
Bedford 1857	22	17	—	—
Beverley 1840	33	56	—	—
Beverley 1859	55	37	26	—
Bristol 1832	99	125	129	—
Bristol 1837	174	137	—	97
Bristol 1841	210	136	—	105
Bristol 1852	168	71	—	—
Cambridge 1835	33	16	31	—
Cambridge 1840	31	24	—	—
Cambridge 1845	29	30	—	—
Cambridge 1857	28	25	28	24
Cambridge 1859	25	17	25	16
Cambridge 1863	21	21	—	—
Cambridge 1865	23	20	23	20
Cambridge 1866	36	35	—	—
Cambridge 1868	121	63	—	—
Chatham 1857	25	18	—	—
Chatham 1859	19	14	—	—
Ipswich 1832	27	11	27	9
Ipswich 1835	17	13	17	12
Ipswich 1847	28	18	25	14
Ipswich 1852	30	18	29	16
Ipswich 1859	33	21	26	16
Ipswich 1865	31	16	—	—
Ipswich 1868	134	37	—	—
Leeds 1834	27	8	—	—
Leicester 1832	43	35	43	—
Leicester 1847	62	44	62	—
Leicester 1859	33	13	31	—
Lewes 1837	27	18	—	—

The voting of shoemakers, 1830–72 (cont.)

Election	Leading Liberal	Leading Tory	Second Liberal	Second Tory
Lewes 1841	29	18	26	26
Maidstone 1857	37	30	34	29
Maidstone 1859	42	21	41	21
Maidstone 1865	41	30	—	—
Northampton 1831	221	52	216	—
Northamptonshire 1831	89	28	88	14
Norwich 1830	125	88	—	—
Oldham 1865	19	9	—	—
Rochdale 1841	11	3	—	—
Rochdale 1857	13	5	—	—
Rochester 1835	25	29	23	—
Rochester 1852	28	23	28	23
Rochester 1856	29	17	—	—
Rochester 1859	23	18	22	17
Rochester 1865	19	11	17	—
Rochester 1868	25	12	—	—
Sandwich 1868	35	15	31	—
Shrewsbury 1857	40	19	—	—
Shrewsbury 1868	101	92	50	—
Shropshire 1832	22	16	—	6
Tamworth 1837	17	20	—	5
Wakefield 1837	12	7	—	—
Warrington 1847	9	4	—	—
York 1835	127	124	104	—
York 1852	94	96	80	—

6. The voting of butchers and grocers, 1830–72

N.B. Only those cases where there was a significant divergence of pattern are shown below.

Election	Leading Liberal	Leading Tory	Second Liberal	Second Tory
Ashton 1841				
Butchers	6	8	—	—
Other retailers	80	48	—	—
Bedford 1841				
Butchers	10	16	—	—
Grocers	11	10	—	—
Bedford 1857				
Butchers	11	10	—	—
Grocers	16	6	—	—
Cambridge 1835				
Butchers	6	17	3	—
Grocers	21	12	21	—

The voting of butchers and grocers, 1830–72 (cont.)

Election	Leading Liberal	Leading Tory	Second Liberal	Second Tory
Cambridge 1840				
Butchers	2	18	—	—
Grocers	19	15	—	—
Cambridge 1845				
Butchers	3	23	—	—
Grocers	26	17	—	—
Cambridge 1857				
Butchers	4	19	3	16
Grocers	25	17	23	16
Cambridge 1859				
Butchers	7	15	7	13
Grocers	21	20	21	20
Cambridge 1863				
Butchers	4	13	—	—
Grocers	21	12	—	—
Cambridge 1865				
Butchers	8	13	7	11
Grocers	34	13	31	13
Cambridge 1866				
Butchers	9	21	—	—
Grocers	43	21	—	—
Cambridge 1868				
Butchers	12	32	—	—
Grocers	53	22	—	—
Chatham 1857				
Butchers	13	20	—	—
Grocers	29	18	—	—
Chatham 1859				
Butchers	14	19	—	—
Grocers	28	20	—	—
Dover 1833				
Butchers	5	24	—	—
Grocers	15	17	—	—
Dover 1837				
Butchers	10	19	—	14
Grocers	24	15	—	11
Halifax* 1847				
Butchers	1	7	1	6
All retailers	82	63	79	55
Leicester 1847				
Butchers	23	36	23	—
Grocers	66	31	63	—

* In the case of Halifax, the Whig candidate is counted as a Tory, and the two Radical candidates counted as the Liberals.

The voting of butchers and grocers, 1830–72 (cont.)

Election	Leading Liberal	Leading Tory	Second Liberal	Second Tory
Liverpool 1832				
Butchers	58	47	48	29
Grocers	53	19	42	10
Maidstone 1857				
Butchers	13	22	11	20
Grocers	37	13	39	10
Northampton 1852				
Butchers	21	29	18	—
Grocers	11	11	12	—
Northamptonshire 1831				
Butchers	75	59	58	34
Grocers	60	24	52	15
Rochdale 1841				
Butchers	14	11	—	—
Grocers	58	22	—	—
Rochdale 1857				
Butchers	16	25	—	—
Grocers	71	37	—	—
Rochester 1852				
Butchers	11	17	11	17
Grocers	22	12	22	12
Rochester 1856				
Butchers	14	13	—	—
Grocers	19	9	—	—
Sandwich 1852				
Butchers	2	15	—	—
Grocers	13	9	—	—
Sandwich 1859				
Butchers	10	14	11	9
Grocers	21	8	21	8
Sandwich 1868				
Butchers	10	21	11	—
Grocers	22	12	22	—
Shrewsbury 1857				
Butchers	10	21	—	—
Grocers	36	10	—	—
Warrington 1847				
Butchers	4	11	—	—
Other retailers	83	50	—	—

N.B. In some minor cases (Beverley 1859, Lewes 1841, Lincoln 1848), butchers were more Liberal than grocers. In some more important cases (Bristol 1841), they voted almost exactly alike. These exceptions however are sufficiently rare to make the selective table above quite a fair indication of the general picture.

The voting of butchers and grocers, 1830–72 (cont.)

It is curious to note a remarkable difference in suicide rates between the two occupations at this time:

> Suicides among males of 25–65 years,
> per million
>
> | | |
> |---|---|
> | General average | 222 |
> | Grocers | 218 |
> | Butchers | 407 |

(Mulhall, *Dictionary of Statistics*, 4th ed., 1899, p. 552.)

7. The voting of gentlemen, 1830–72: some characteristic cases

Election	Leading Liberal	Leading Tory	Second Liberal	Second Tory
Bedford 1857	24	22	—	—
Bolton 1835	23	26	15	—
Brighton 1841	42	23	33	—
Bristol 1837	131	283	277	—
Bristol 1852	127	225	—	—
Cambridge 1835	50	41	50	—
Cambridge 1845	47	33	—	—
Cambridge 1857	42	51	38	48
Cambridge 1866	37	61	—	—
Cambridge 1868	61	78	—	—
Chatham 1857	45	45	—	—
Chatham 1859	45	33	—	—
Dover 1833	46	46	—	—
Ipswich 1832	45	29	43	25
Ipswich 1852	46	67	41	64
Ipswich 1865	86	81	—	—
Ipswich 1868	118	100	—	—
Lancaster 1865	17	25	—	—
Leicester 1832	43	71	28	—
Lewes 1841	21	24	21	24
Liverpool 1832	128	84	107	61
Maidstone 1832	35	29	—	—
Maidstone 1859	32	46	31	49
Maidstone 1865	38	45	—	—
Maidstone 1870	41	50	—	—
Northamptonshire 1831	223	169	205	117
Norwich 1830	112	124	115	122
Oldham 1865	7	34	—	—
Rochdale 1841	6	22	—	—
Rochester 1852	42	43	42	43
Rochester 1856	47	32	—	—
Rochester 1868	59	21	—	—
Sandwich 1868	72	53	68	—
Shrewsbury 1857	31	37	—	—
Shrewsbury 1868	71	77	10	—
Wakefield 1837	22	14	—	—
Warrington 1847	13	14	—	—

8. The voting of publicans and beersellers, 1852-72

Election	Leading Liberal	Leading Tory	Second Liberal	Second Tory
Bedford 1857				
Publicans	22	21	—	—
Bristol 1852				
Publicans	118	71	—	—
Beersellers	108	32	—	—
Cambridge 1857				
Publicans	25	33	27	32
Cambridge 1865				
Publicans	40	41	39	39
Cambridge 1866				
Publicans	30	38	—	—
Cambridge 1868				
Publicans	41	40	—	—
Chatham 1857				
Publicans	38	58	—	—
Chatham 1859				
Publicans	41	56	—	—
Ipswich 1852				
Publicans	25	37	24	32
Ipswich 1859				
Publicans	39	78	13	76
Ipswich 1865				
Publicans	36	71	—	—
Ipswich 1868				
Publicans	15	71	—	—
Beersellers	10	19	—	—
Leicester 1861				
Publicans	29	28	2	—
Maidstone 1857				
Publicans	16	26	14	24
Beersellers	6	14	5	12
Maidstone 1859				
Publicans	17	25	16	26
Beersellers	7	17	7	17
Maidstone 1865				
Publicans	22	33	—	—
Beersellers	14	21	—	—
Maidstone 1870				
Publicans	19	25	—	—
Beersellers	5	19	—	—
Oldham 1865				
Publicans	41	80	—	—
Beersellers	30	74	—	—
Rochdale 1857				
Publicans	10	46	—	—
Beersellers	16	63	—	—

The voting of publicans and beersellers, 1852–72 (cont.)

Election	Leading Liberal	Leading Tory	Second Liberal	Second Tory
Rochester 1852				
Publicans	25	17	25	17
Rochester 1868				
Beersellers	11	8	—	—
Publicans	33	17	—	—
Sandwich 1868				
Publicans	46	48	45	—
Shrewsbury 1857				
Publicans	53	32	—	—
Shrewsbury 1868				
Publicans	57	65	9	—
Beersellers	17	19	7	—

9. The voting of pilots, 1830–72

Election	Leading Liberal	Leading Tory	Second Liberal	Second Tory
Bristol 1837	1	3	—	0
Bristol 1841	1	3	—	3
Dover 1832	11	33	3	12
Dover 1833	9	29	—	—
Dover 1835	8	15	—	39
Dover 1837	8	36	—	28
Ipswich 1847	1	3	0	4
Ipswich 1852	0	3	0	3
Ipswich 1857	0	4	0	4
Ipswich 1859	0	4	0	4
Liverpool 1830	9	39	—	—
Liverpool 1832	11	34	6	23
Liverpool 1835	6	33	1	28
Liverpool 1841	2	65	1	65
Rochester 1835	2	1	2	—
Rochester 1852	1	1	0	1
Rochester 1856	0	1	—	—
Rochester 1859	1	1	1	1
Sandwich 1852	1	45	—	—
Sandwich 1859	26	11	24	7
Sandwich 1868	34	20	33	—
Yarmouth 1832	6	11	6	—
Yarmouth 1838	4	5	—	—
Yarmouth 1841	2	8	2	8
Yarmouth 1847	1	7	1	7

10. The voting of Dissenting ministers, 1830–47

Election	Leading Liberal	Leading Tory	Second Liberal	Second Tory
Abingdon 1830	2	o	—	—
Beverley 1840	2	o	—	—
Beverley 1847	1	o	2	—
Bolton 1832	3	o	3	—
Bolton 1835	o	o	4	o
Bolton 1837	4	1	4	—
Brighton 1837	6	1	6	—
Brighton 1841	3	2	3	—
Bristol 1837	9	o	—	o
Bristol 1841	14	o	—	o
Cambridge 1835	2	o	2	o
Cambridge 1840	1	o	—	—
Cambridge 1845	5	o	—	—
Dover 1832	1	o	1	o
Dover 1833	1	o	—	—
Dover 1835	1	1	—	o
Dover 1837	1	o	o	—
Durham 1832	1	o	1	—
Hereford 1832	1	o	1	—
Hereford 1835	2	o	2	—
Ipswich 1832	3	o	2	o
Ipswich 1835	3	o	3	o
Ipswich 1847	8	o	8	o
Leeds 1834	2	o	—	—
Leicester 1832	5	o	5	o
Leicester 1847	6	1	6	—
Leicestershire 1830	13	4	—	2
Lewes 1835	4	o	4	o
Lewes 1837	4	1	—	—
Lewes 1841	2	1	2	1
Lindsey 1835	5	1	9	—
Lindsey 1852	3	o	—	o
Liverpool 1835	13	2	13	1
Liverpool 1841	13	o	13	o
Maidstone 1832	3	o	—	—
Maidstone 1841	3	o	—	o
Manchester 1839	8	o	—	—
Northampton 1831	6	o	6	o
Northamptonshire 1831	20	o	19	o
Norwich 1830	2	o	1	o
Preston 1841	4	o	3	o
Reading 1837	4	o	4	o
Reading 1841	2	1	2	1
Shrewsbury 1837	3	o	3	o

The voting of Dissenting ministers, 1830–47 (cont.)

Election	Leading Liberal	Leading Tory	Second Liberal	Second Tory
Shrewsbury 1847	1	0	0	—
Shrewsbury 1868	8	0	6	—
Tamworth 1841	1	0	0	0
Tewkesbury 1831	1	0	2	0
Tewkesbury 1841	3	0	3	—
Wakefield 1837	1	0	—	—
York 1835	3	0	3	0

11. The voting of Dissenting ministers, 1848–72

Election	Leading Liberal	Leading Tory	Second Liberal	Second Tory
Beverley 1854	1	0	—	—
Bristol 1852	14	1	—	—
Bury St Edmunds 1852	3	3	—	0
Cambridge 1857	2	0	2	0
Cambridge 1859	2	0	2	0
Cambridge 1865	3	0	2	0
Cambridge 1868	6	0	6	0
Chatham 1857	3	0	—	—
Chatham 1859	1	0	—	—
Ipswich 1852	6	0	6	0
Ipswich 1857	7	0	7	0
Ipswich 1859	7	0	4	0
Ipswich 1865	9	0	—	—
Ipswich 1868	9	0	—	—
Leicester 1859	10	1	4	0
Leicester 1861	14	2	1	—
Maidstone 1853	6	—	0	—
Maidstone 1857	2	0	2	0
Maidstone 1859	3	0	3	0
Maidstone 1865	7	0	—	—
Maidstone 1870	7	0	—	—
Nottingham 1852	5	2	0	—
Oldham 1865	3	0	—	—
Rochester 1852	1	0	1	0
Rochester 1859	2	0	2	0
Rochester 1865	1	0	1	0
Rochester 1868	1	0	—	—
Sandwich 1852	4	0	—	—
Sandwich 1859	5	1	6	1
Sandwich 1868	4	0	4	—
York 1852	3	0	0	—

12. The voting of Dissenting ministers: specific denominations

Election	Leading Liberal	Leading Tory	Second Liberal	Second Tory
Independent* ministers				
Beverley 1854	1	0	—	—
Manchester 1839	3	0	—	—
Tewkesbury 1841	1	0	1	0
Methodists				
Cambridge 1868	2†	0	2†	0
Liverpool 1832	0	1†	—	—
Bristol 1837	1	0	—	0
Bristol 1841	1†	0	—	0
Bristol 1841	1	0	—	0
Leeds 1834	1	0	—	—
Leicester 1859	1	0	0	0
Maidstone 1832	1†	0	—	—
Baptist preachers, ministers				
Bristol 1841	1	0	—	0
Leicester 1859	1	1	0	0
Manchester 1839	2	0	—	—
Tewkesbury 1841	2	0	2	—
Cambridge 1868	2	0	2	0
Unitarian ministers				
Manchester 1839	3	0	—	—
Presbyterian ministers				
Rochester 1868	1	0	—	—

* I.e. Congregationalist, presumably.   † Wesleyan.

13. 'The Political Sentiments of Wesleyans', 1841(?)* (extract)

'We continue to cherish the hope of being able to ascertain the political sentiments of our Wesleyan brethren as evinced by their votes at elections for the boroughs and counties in which they possess the elective franchise. From time to time the kindness of correspondents has enabled us to state in what way Wesleyan voters have in particular places disposed of their suffrages. We have been at the pains of collecting these accounts and of registering the results which they disclose in a tabular form. These returns comprise 29 cities and boroughs, and 7 county districts, of which 4 belong to the West Riding of Yorkshire. They exhibit, as nearly as can be ascertained, the number of Wesleyan electors in each place, and the manner in which they voted at the last Election.

Place	Total no. of Wesleyan Voters	Voted Liberal	Voted Tory	Split Votes	Abstained
Durham	23	21	2	0	0
Kendal	15	14	0	0	1
Salisbury	53	47	1	0	5

* This excerpt from the *Wesleyan Chronicle* is to be found in *The League*, vol. 1, no. 44 (27 July 1844), p. 720. The reference was given me by Dr Brian Harrison, Fellow of Nuffield College, Oxford.

F

'*The Political Sentiments of Wesleyans*' (*cont.*)

Place	Total no. of Wesleyan Voters	Voted Liberal	Voted Tory	Split Votes	Abstained
Leicester	66	60	6	0	0
Exeter	90	85	3	2	0
Rochester	74	44	18	7	5
Plymouth	73	60	10	3	0
Lancaster	33	27	2	2	2
Rochdale	130	105	15	0	10
Aylesbury	30	11	17	0	2
Newport, I.o.W.	52	36	15	0	1
Bury St Edmunds	25	17	6	0	2
Canterbury	45	27	10	4	4
Norwich	80	63	12	0	3
Oxford	82	58	14	4	6
Stroud	46	32	1	0	13
Taunton	34	22	8	0	4
Halifax	81	49	21	5	6
Thetford	16	9	0	7	0
Frome	33	20	10	0	3
Worcester	61	52	6	3	0
Northampton	113	87	19	4	3
Maidstone	41	25	16	0	0
Derby	63	51	9	0	3
Kidderminster	24	17	2	0	5
Leeds (Bramley township)	117	86	20	0	11
Yarmouth	111	84	10	1	16
Ludlow	22	14	7	0	1
Banbury	31	21	7	0	3
Mildenhall	25	24	0	1	0
Wednesbury	48	34	12	1	1
Settle	12	11	0	0	1
Dent, Yorks.	29	10	14	0	5
Addingham, Yorks.	27	20	4	0	3
Oulton, Yorks.	16	7	7	2	0
Bury, Lancs.	24	20	4	0	0
Total	1843	1370	308	46	119

...We ourselves, however, shall not rest satisfied until we are able to present our readers with a table showing how the Wesleyans have voted in each borough and county of the United Kingdom. Our friends are therefore earnestly entreated to supply us as quickly as possible with the needful information.'

(*Wesleyan Chronicle*)

B. CONSTITUENCIES ANALYSED BY OCCUPATIONS

The Abingdon election of 30 July 1830

The pollbook is in the Bodleian Library.

Result: Maberly, Whig   159
Maitland, Tory   94

All voters	Maberly	Maitland	All voters	Maberly	Maitland
Clergymen	1	1	Cordwainers	8	3
Surgeons	4	1	Ironfounders	0	2
Gentlemen	11	8	Sheriff's officer	0	1
Bakers	10	8	Parish clerk	0	1
Dissenting ministers	2	0	Labourer	0	1
Lawyer	1	0	Miller	0	2
Victuallers	20	15	Tailors	6	1
Butchers	9	1	Farmer	1	0
Grocers	6	3	Banker	1	0
Carpenters	3	1	Others	76	45

The Ashton-under-Lyne election of 1841

The pollbook is in Ashton-under-Lyne Public Library.

Result: Hindley, Charles   Liberal   303
Harrop, Jonah   Conservative   254

All voters	Harrop	Hindley	All voters	Harrop	Hindley
I. Gentlemen	7	5	V. Cottonmasters	4	9
Legal	5	1	Overlookers	3	7
Medical	4	4	Textile	34	33
Official	7	1	workers		
Other professionals	13	14	VI. Small business	6	18
II. Publicans	22	11	Ironfounders	2	3
Beersellers	20	13	Clerks	8	4
Brewer	1	0	VII. Metal, engineering	12	9
III. Butchers	8	6	Tailors	4	6
Other shopkeepers	48	80	Shoemakers	8	20
			Building crafts	10	16
IV. Labourers, etc.	10	13	Other artisans	5	9

Summary

		Conservative	Liberal
I.	Gentlemen, Professions	36	25
II.	Drink	43	24
III.	Retailers	56	86
IV.	Labourers	10	13
V.	Cotton	41	49
VI.	Small business	16	25
VII.	Artisans	39	60

The Aylesbury election of May 1831

The pollbook, which is in the Institute of Historical Research, gives the occupations of the electors of Aylesbury town only, and not of the electors from the surrounding hundreds who made up the bulk of the constituency.

Result: Wm. Rickford   983
        Lord Nugent   604
        Lord Kirkwall   508

Rickford and Nugent were the Reform candidates. Kirkwall was the nominee of Lords Chandos and Buckingham, who also ordered their faggot voters to support Rickford in the hope of excluding Nugent.

Selected categories	Nugent	Rickford	Kirkwall
Gentlemen	7	9	3
Clergymen	2	2	0
Minister	1	1	0
Surgeons	3	2	0
Attorney	0	1	1
Victuallers	7	14	7
Grocers	5	7	1
Butchers	6	12	6
Tailors	12	15	4
Cordwainers	20	27	12
Labourers	23	46	25

The Banbury election of 1847

The pollbook is in the Bodleian Library.

Result: H. W. Tancred, Liberal   226
        J. Macgregor, Conservative   164

Selected categories	Tancred	Macgregor
Grocers	7	6
Butchers	7	6
Tailors	10	5
Shoemakers	12	1
Lawyers	6	4
Gentlemen	14	6
Farmers	4	13
Surgeons	2	3
Dissenting ministers	2	1
Banker	1	0
Saddlers	3	2
Sexton	1	0
Police officer	0	1

The Bath election of 1847

The pollbook is in the Bodleian Library.

Result: Lord Ashley, Conservative   1,278
        Lord Duncan, Liberal   1,228
        J. A. Roebuck, Radical   1,093

Voters A–Z

Selected categories	Roebuck	Duncan	Ashley
R.C. priest	1	1	0
Sweeps	1	1	7
Unitarian ministers	1	2	0
Clergymen	2	3	44
Surgeons	10	20	48
Beersellers	26	24	5
Labourers	18	21	14
Army	4	5	20
Navy	5	7	11
Bankers	0	4	4
Saddlers	2	2	8
Postboys	0	1	3

Voters A–J inclusive only*

Selected categories	Roebuck	Duncan	Ashley
Grocers	25	24	14
Butchers	18	21	14
Policemen	2	3	4
Gentlemen	49	65	91
Victuallers	24	27	15
Tailors	27	28	16
Wesleyan preacher	1	1	0
Shoemakers	24	28	18

* I.e. half the electorate.

The Bedford election of 1841

The pollbook is in Bedford Public Library.

Result: F. Polhill, Conservative   433
        Capt. Henry Stuart, Conservative 421
        W. H. Whitbread, Liberal   410

Votes analysed were *only* (a) the 349 plumpers for Whitbread, and (b) the 393 who split between Polhill and Stuart.

		Liberal	Con-servative			Liberal	Con-servative
I.	Gentlemen	8	16		Officials	3	2
	Farmers	6	7		Teachers and clergy	3	10
II.	Legal	2	3		Other pro-fessions	5	4
	Medical	8	7				
	Military	1	5				
	Clerks	5	11	III.	Miscellaneous	9	8

The Bedford election of 1841 (cont.)

		Liberal	Con-servative			Liberal	Con-servative
IV.	Publicans	13	15		Bakers	16	10
					Butchers	10	16
V.	Millers and maltsters	2	4		Others	17	16
	Merchants	4	5	VII.	Servants	14	18
	Banker	1	1		Labourers	56	46
	Builder	0	1	VIII.	Building	38	44
	Brewers	4	9		Metal	18	23
					Shoemakers	28	36
VI.	Grocers	11	10		Tailors	23	17
	Drapers	14	12		Others	26	36

Summary:		Liberal	Conservative
I.	Gentlemen	14	23
II.	Professions	27	42
III.	Miscellaneous	9	8
IV.	Publicans	13	15
V.	Business	11	20
VI.	Retail	68	64
VII.	Labour	70	64
VIII.	Crafts	133	156

The Bedford election of 1857

The pollbook is in Bedford Public Library.

Result: Samuel Whitbread, Liberal	452
Thos. Barnard, Liberal	435
Wm. Stuart, Conservative	376
E. T. Smith, Conservative	176

Votes analysed were (*a*) the 399 votes split between Whitbread and Barnard and (*b*) plumpers for Stuart (136), for Smith (5), and splitters for Stuart and Smith (164)—in all 305 Tory voters analysed.

		Liberal	Con-servative			Liberal	Con-servative
I.	Gentlemen	24	22	V.	Brewers	5	9
	Farmers	7	6		Builders	5	6
II.	Legal	3	5		Banker	1	0
	Medical	3	6		Millers and maltsters	8	3
	Military	4	6		Small mfr.	1	1
	Clerks	6	15		Coal merchants	5	3
	Teachers and clergy	10	5		Merchants	5	6
	Miscellaneous	10	5				
	Officials	6	1	VI.	Railway employees	5	0
	Musicians	0	2		Labourers	17	23
III.	Miscellaneous	13	10		Servants	15	3
IV.	Publicans	22	21				

The Bedford election of 1857 (cont.)

		Liberal	Con-servative			Liberal	Con-servative
VII.	Grocers	16	6	VIII.	Building	31	28
	Drapers	22	2		Metal	21	19
	Butchers	11	10		Shoemakers	22	17
	Bakers	16	8		Tailors	26	9
	Others	22	16		Others	35	27

Summary		Liberal	Conservative
I.	Gentlemen	31	28
II.	Professions	42	45
III.	Miscellaneous	13	10
IV.	Publicans	22	21
V.	Business	30	28
VI.	Labour	37	26
VII.	Retail	87	42
VIII.	Craftsmen	135	100

The Beverley election of 31 July 1830

The pollbook is in the Guildhall Library.*

Result: Henry Burton, Whig   1,065
Daniel Sykes, Whig   739
Capel Cure, Tory   657

Capel Cure was an Essex country gentleman, and Daniel Sykes, formerly an iron merchant in Hull, had become its Recorder.

Selected categories	Burton	Sykes	Cure
Innkeepers	23	14	17
Cordwainers	113	52	78
Mariners	27	12	20
Gentlemen	40	36	20
Butchers	45	50	23
Grocers	27	25	6
Shipwrights	15	9	7
Farmers	24	30	6
Labourers	39	19	21
Surgeons	6	4	5
Parish clerk	1	2	1
Shipowner	0	1	0
Banker	0	1	0
Weavers	15	5	7
Merchants	3	5	3
Watermen	3	1	3
Gaolers	2	1	1
Sexton	0	0	1
Clergymen	1	0	1

* This refers throughout to the Guildhall Library in the City of London.

The Beverley election of 1840

The pollbook is in the Guildhall Library.

Result: Sackville Lane Fox, Conservative   556
Thomas Murray, Liberal   410

Selected categories	Murray	Fox
Solicitors	4	5
Surgeons	4	4
Farmers	11	48
Butchers	19	20
Grocers	6	9
Mariners	8	7
Shoemakers	33	56
Labourers	25	37
Watermen	1	4
Dissenting ministers	2	0
Relieving officer	0	1

The Beverley election of 1847

The pollbook is in Manchester Public Library.

Result: S. L. Fox, Protectionist   543
J. Towneley, Liberal   542
Sir I. Goldsmid, Liberal   257

Selected categories	Towneley	Goldsmid	Fox
Gentlemen	15	11	40
Solicitors	2	1	5
Surgeons	2	0	3
Clergymen	1	1	3
Parish clerk	1	0	1
Butchers	19	6	20
Wesleyan minister	0	0	1
Dissenting ministers	1	2	0
Farmers	21	6	48

The Beverley election of 1854

The pollbook is in the Guildhall Library.

Result: Hon. Arthur Gordon, Liberal   493
G. W. Hastings, Conservative   192

Selected categories	Gordon	Hastings
Gentlemen	18	10
Solicitors	0	1
Surgeons	2	0
Farmers	17	7
Butchers	10	2
Grocers	9	3

The Beverley election of 1854 (cont.)

Selected categories	Gordon	Hastings
Mariners	7	2
Shoemakers	41	16
Labourers	30	24
Railwayman	1	0
Sexton	1	0
Registrar	1	0
R.C. priest	1	0
Independent minister	1	0

The Beverley by-election of 1857

The pollbook is in Manchester Public Library.

Result: Henry Edwards, Conservative   579
William Wells, Liberal   401

Selected categories	Wells	Edwards
Gentlemen	12	51
Solicitors	1	4
Surgeons	2	2
Clergymen	0	3
Farmers	23	37
Gaoler	1	0

The Beverley election of 1859

The pollbook is in the Guildhall Library.

Result: Ralph Walters, Liberal   605
Henry Edwards, Conservative   539
J. R. Walker, Conservative   435
E. A. Glover, Liberal-Conservative   54

Selected categories	Walters	Edwards	Walker
Solicitors	0	5	3
Surgeons	3	2	1
Clergy	0	3	3
Farmers	17	36	31
Butchers	16	5	5
Grocers	12	15	12
Mariners	12	12	9
Shoemakers	55	37	26
Labourers	53	36	25
Railwaymen	2	1	0
Gentlemen	21	51	43
Sexton	1	0	0
Organists	0	2	1
Dissenting ministers	3	1	1

The Birmingham Liberal caucus in 1880

The apparently socially exclusive character of the Birmingham radical caucus is strongly suggested by this analysis of activists in the Market Hall Ward. Materials also exist for a social analysis of Edgbaston Ward party, but this was not pursued as the essential point about the gentility of radicalism is better made in relation to the very mixed and not specially genteel Market Hall Ward in the town centre.

Members representing the Ward on the City Executive Committee, and also Ward Executive Committee:

President. A merchant
Treasurer. A merchant
Secretary. A merchant
Businessman
Ironmonger
Accountant and estate agent

Ward representatives on the '800' (the caucus): 50 persons

Businessmen and merchants	4	Bootmaker	1
Coal merchants	2	Pawnbroker	1
Solicitors	4	Silk mercer	1
Accountants	3	Drapers	2
Stockbroker	1	Saddler	1
Auctioneer	1	Master decorator	1
Maltster	1	Master tailors	2
Estate agent	1	Wholesale baker	1
Doctor	1	Antique dealer	1
Grammar school teachers*	2	Publican	1
Law stationer	1	Hotelier	1
Watchmaker	1	Manager, Coffee House Co.	1
Ironmonger	1	Occupation not discoverable	13

* One of these was a clergyman.

Sources: *Birmingham Liberal Association, Market Hall Ward. List of officers,* etc. (1880) (Birmingham Public Library, reference no. 72349), and *Birmingham Directory,* 1880.

The Bolton election of 1835

The pollbook is in the Guildhall Library.

Result: Wm. Bolling, Conservative   633
Peter Ainsworth, Liberal   590
Robert Torrens, Liberal   343

Selected categories	Ainsworth	Torrens	Bolling
Beersellers	32	5	29
Surgeons	9	7	15
Spinners	14	11	30
Cloggers	12	6	4
Publicans	40	15	46
Weavers	10	4	9
Tailors	12	5	10
Grocers	10	5	7

The Bolton election of 1835 (cont.)

Selected categories	Ainsworth	Torrens	Bolling
Farmers	15	2	16
Butchers	13	12	13
Ironfounders	9	1	13
Manufacturers	44	41	37
Labourer	1	0	1
Gentlemen	23	15	26
Bleachers	3	3	6
Paper makers	2	1	1
Machine makers	1	0	2
Shoemakers	10	7	12
Overlookers	2	3	7
Manager	1	0	1
Spindle makers	3	0	3
Foundrymen	1	0	2
Solicitors	6	5	12
Collier	1	0	1
Mechanics	2	1	6
Clergymen	2	0	3
Sizers	3	0	1
Cotton dealers	2	1	3
Calenderer	1	0	1
Boilermakers	0	2	4
Coalmasters	0	0	8
Dissenting ministers	0	4	0
Moulder	0	1	1
Banker	0	0	1
Warper	1	1	0

The Boston election of 1852

The pollbook is in the Bodleian Library.

Result: Heathcote, Liberal 547
Cabbell, Conservative 490
J. A. Hankey, Liberal 436
T. Hankey, Liberal 146
Adams, Conservative 19

Selected categories	Heathcote	J. Hankey	T. Hankey	Cabbell
Railwaymen	6	11	6	4
Shoemakers	25	10	4	29
Policemen	2	1	0	2
Pilots	4	5	1	2
Wesleyan minister	0	0	0	1
Sexton	1	0	0	1
Bankers	3	1	1	2
Baptist minister	0	1	1	0
Anglican clergy	1	0	0	2
Independent minister	1	1	0	0

According to the pollbook, 'since the Reform Act little personal influence has prevailed'.

The Brighton election of 1832

The pollbook, which is in the Guildhall Library, takes the form of a single alphabetical list.

Result: I. N. Wigney, Liberal 873
G. Faithfull, Liberal 722
Capt. Pechell, R.N., Liberal 613
Wm. Crawford, Liberal 391
Sir A. J. Dalrymple, Conservative 32

Voters A–D inclusive only

	Wigney	Faithfull	Pechell	Crawford
Gentlemen	26	17	36	26

Voters A–Z

Selected categories	Wigney	Faithfull	Pechell	Crawford
Clergy	0	0	12	10
Officers	1	0	11	5
Sexton	1	0	0	1
Dissenting ministers	4	3	1	2
Carpenters	52	63	21	14
Butchers	30	25	17	10
Shoemakers	36	36	7	8
Grocers	53	48	15	9
Surgeons	5	1	31	25
Saddlers	5	2	4	5
Beersellers	5	11	2	3
Mariners	2	1	1	0
Publicans	30	19	17	3
Bankers	0	1	2	2
Labourers	10	10	5	2
Police	2	1	1	0

The Brighton election of 1835

The pollbook is in the Library of the Society of Genealogists.

Result: Capt. G. R. Pechell, Liberal 961
I. W. Wigney, Liberal 523
Sir Adolphus Dalrymple, Cons. 483
Geo. Faithfull, Liberal 467

Selected categories	Pechell	Wigney	Faithfull	Dalrymple
Anglican clergy	12	2	0	11
Parish clerks	2	0	0	2
Sexton	1	0	0	1
Dissenting ministers	0	5	4	1
Officers	7	3	0	3
Surgeons	29	9	1	17
Lawyers	16	5	4	10
Gentlemen	200	107	47	112
Cordwainers	18	10	18	10
Carpenters	34	18	46	12
Beersellers	11	1	7	2

The Brighton election of 1837

The pollbook is in the Institute of Historical Research.

Result: Capt. G. R. Pechell, R.N., Liberal   1,083
Sir Adolphus J. Dalrymple, Bt., Cons.   819
I. N. Wigney, Liberal   801
Geo. Faithfull, Liberal   183

Selected categories	Pechell	Wigney	Faithfull	Dalrymple
Clergymen	5	3	1	18
Parish clerk	1	0	0	1
Sexton	1	0	0	1
Dissenting ministers	6	6	0	1
Bankers	2	1	0	3
Officers	5	3	0	8
Surgeons	18	9	1	19
Organist	1	0	0	1
Butchers	32	21	4	31
Grocers	46	44	14	30
Carpenters	62	40	17	42
Fishermen	3	2	1	2
Mariners	5	2	0	5
Labourers	12	4	4	12

Plumps		Splits	
Wigney	39	Wigney and Pechell	616
Pechell	30	Wigney and Dalrymple	102
Dalrymple	268	Wigney and Faithfull	44
Faithfull	51	Pechell and Dalrymple	399
		Pechell and Faithfull	38
		Dalrymple and Faithfull	50

The Brighton election of 1841

The pollbook, which is in the Guildhall Library, takes the form of a single alphabetical list. Result: Pechell, Liberal   1,443
Wigney, Liberal   1,235
Dalrymple, Conservative 872
C. Brooker, Liberal   19

Voters A–D inclusive only

	Pechell	Wigney	Dalrymple
Gentlemen	42	33	23

Voters A–Z

Selected categories	Pechell	Wigney	Dalrymple
Ministers	3	3	2
Clergy	6	6	21
Sexton	0	0	1
Butchers	46	44	26
Grocers	56	50	23
Carpenters	91	71	43

The Brighton election of 1841 (cont.)

Voters A–Z (*cont.*)

Selected categories	Pechell	Wigney	Dalrymple
Saddlers	8	9	5
Officers	5	5	5
Surgeons	17	15	20
Labourers	29	19	16
Bankers	0	0	2
R.C. priest	1	1	0
Police	2	2	2
Parish clerk	1	0	1

The Bristol election of 30 July–5 August 1830

The pollbook is in the Institute of Historical Research.

Result: R. Hart Davis (probably Ministerialist)   5,012
James Evan Baillie (West India interest Whig)   3,377
Edward Protheroe (anti-slavery and Reform)   2,840
Jas. Acland (Radical)   25

Selected categories excluding out-voters*	Davis	Protheroe	Baillie
Colliers	13	2	17
Subsacrist	1	0	0
Organists	2	2	1
Cathedral almsmen	2	0	2
Dissenting ministers	0	2	0
Anglican clergy	19	5	16
Victuallers	47	25	24
Merchants	42	20	29
Mariners	84	28	85
Cordwainers	265	133	174
Labourers	271	121	198
Shipwrights	128	16	127

Davis: plumps   183
            and Baillie   2,900
            and Protheroe   1,929
                                        ───
                                       5,012

Baillie: plumps   460
            and Davis   2,900
            and Protheroe   15
            and Acland   2
                                        ───
                                       3,377

Protheroe: plumps   873
               and Davis   1,929
               and Baillie   15
               and Acland   23
                                        ───
                                       2,840

Acland: and Protheroe   23
             and Baillie   2
                                         ──
                                         25

* Out-voters were about one-sixth of the electorate.

The Bristol election of 1830 (cont.)

The pollbook quotes Charles Pinney as saying in support of J. E. Baillie, the pro-slavery Whig: 'Gentlemen, the present Election differs in principle and public importance from any that has previously occurred in this city. So great is the difference, that the old party names are either forgotten, or in disuse, and for the first time, a new distinction has taken place. Slavery and Anti-Slavery is now the cry, instead of Whig and Tory...I believe I do not exaggerate when I assert that ⅝ of the whole trade of Bristol depend on the West Indies.'

The Bristol election of December 1832

The pollbook is in the Institute of Historical Research, and lists the occupations of freemen voters only.

Result: Sir Richard Vyvyan, Conservative 3,709
   J. E. Baillie, Liberal 3,159
   Edward Protheroe, Liberal 3,030
   John Williams, Liberal 2,741

Freemen only: selected categories	Baillie	Protheroe	Williams	Vyvyan
Colliers	5	16	16	5
Surgeons	7	2	2	12
Organists	1	1	1	1
Subsacrist	0	0	0	1
Cathedral almsmen	1	0	0	2
Parish clerk	1	0	0	1
Clergy	11	1	1	13
Merchants	34	9	6	31
Grocers	16	10	10	21
Mariners	62	20	19	67
Shipwrights	86	30	25	79
Labourers	142	125	108	191
Cordwainers	99	129	112	125

The Bristol election of 1837

The pollbook is in the Institute of Historical Research.

Result: P. W. S. Miles, Conservative 3,838
  Hon. F. H. F. Berkeley, Liberal 3,212
  Wm. Fripp, Conservative 3,156

Selected categories	Berkeley	Miles	Fripp
Pilots	1	3	0
Colliers	17	14	5
Bankers	2	8	8
Lamplighters	3	2	2
Sextons	1	3	3
Clergy	0	11	11
Police	2	5	6
Weavers	9	9	5

The Bristol election of 1837 (cont.)

Selected categories	Berkeley	Miles	Fripp
Dissenting ministers	8	o	o
Organists	o	2	2
Methodist minister	1	o	o
R.C. priest	1	o	o
Parish clerk	o	1	1
Shipbuilders	4	6	5
Chorister	o	1	1
Gentlemen	131	283	277
Merchants	16	74	74
Lawyers	27	54	55
Surgeons	22	54	55
Shoemakers	174	137	97
Shipwrights	25	84	69
Grocers	72	55	46
Mariners	22	42	31
Labourers	108	140	112

The Bristol election of 1841

The pollbook is in the Institute of Historical Research.

Result: P. W. S. Miles, Conservative   4,193
Hon. F. H. F. Berkeley, Liberal   3,739
Wm. Fripp, Conservative   3,684

Selected categories	Berkeley	Miles	Fripp
Bankers	3	8	7
Gravedigger	1	o	o
Parish clerks	1	3	2
Harbourmaster	o	1	1
Methodist preacher	1	o	o
Wesleyan minister	1	o	o
R.C. priests	2	o	o
Organists	o	6	6
Baptist preacher	1	o	o
'Itinerant preacher'	1	o	o
Subsacrist	o	1	1
Verger	o	1	1
Sextons	o	9	9
'Clerks', Rev., etc.	1	11	11
The Dean of Bristol	1	o	o
Chorister	o	1	1
Dissenting ministers	11	o	o
Sweeps	5	4	3
Coal miners	22	6	4
Weavers	4	3	4
Officers	4	15	15
Lamplighters	1	6	6
Watermen	o	5	5
Mariners	9	23	17

The Bristol election of 1841 (cont.)

Selected categories	Berkeley	Miles	Fripp
Police, all ranks	3	10	14
'Captains'	2	8	9
Postmen	0	2	2
Sailmakers	6	12	9
Boatbuilders	4	2	1
Almsmen	4	1	0
Pilots	1	3	3
Merchants	17	69	66
Lawyers	25	77	77
Surgeons	24	58	57
Victuallers	139	141	109
Beersellers	51	34	25
Carpenters	160	116	103
Shoemakers	210	136	105
Shipwrights	51	91	70
Grocers	83	76	69
Butchers	83	73	61
Labourers	87	104	97

The Bristol election of 1852

The pollbook is in the Institute of Historical Research.

Result: F. H. F. Berkeley, Liberal　　4,642
W. H. G. Langton, Liberal　　4,489
F. A. M'Geachy, Conservative　3,648

There was little cross-voting.

The following analysis of selected categories omits 180 out-voters in Gloucester and Somerset.

Selected categories	Berkeley	M'Geachy
Gentlemen	127	225
Military and naval officers	5	18
Barristers	0	3
Surgeons and physicians	30	50
Bankers	3	6
Share brokers	4	7
Victuallers	118	71
Beersellers	108	32
Shoemakers	168	71
Labourers	69	72
Anglican clergy*	3	56
Dissenting ministers	14	1
R.C. priest	1	0
Sextons	0	6
Organists	0	3
Gravediggers	0	2
Sweeps	3	6
Bargeman	0	1

* The Dean of Bristol voted Liberal, as in 1841.

The Bury St Edmunds election of 1852

The pollbook is in the Guildhall Library.

Result: Earl Jermyn, Conservative   493
J. Stuart, Ministerialist   328
E. Bunbury, Liberal   319

Selected categories	Bunbury	Stuart	Jermyn
Solicitors	7	7	12
Surgeons	1	8	9
Farmers	2	7	7
Parish clerks	0	1	1
Butchers	2	6	1
Grocers	2	6	7
Shoemakers	9	3	7
Labourers	1	0	1
Police	2	1	2
Newspaper owner	1	0	1
Sheriff's officer	1	0	1
Corn inspector	1	0	0
Tobacco manufacturer	1	0	0
Relieving officer	0	1	1
Sexton	1	0	1
Willow manufacturer	1	0	0
Ministers	3	0	3
Tax gatherer	1	0	1
Ironfounders	1	1	2
Registrar	1	0	1

The Cambridge Borough election of 1835

The pollbook is in the Guildhall Library.

Result: Spring Rice, Liberal   736
George Pryme, Liberal   693
J. L. Knight, Conservative   688

Selected categories	Rice	Pryme	Knight
Gentlemen	50	44	41
Solicitors	10	11	9
Surgeons	10	11	8
Farmers	1	1	8
Grocers	21	21	12
Butchers	6	3	17
Servants	7	8	24
College servants	34	34	68
Publicans	59	52	56
Clergy	7	6	10
Labourers	5	4	5
Shoemakers	33	31	16
Gaolers	0	0	2
Sheriff's officers	1	1	2
Dissenting ministers	2	2	0

The Cambridge Borough election of 1840

The pollbook is in the Guildhall Library.

Result: Sir A. C. Grant, Conservative   736
Thomas Starkie, Liberal   651

Selected categories	Starkie	Grant
Solicitors	8	8
Surgeons	9	8
Farmers	1	6
Butchers	2	18
Grocers	19	15
Labourers	6	11
College servants	24	69
Servants	5	7
Publicans	36	37
Gentlemen	31	47
Clergy	4	7
Shoemakers	31	24
Parish clerks	0	3
Dissenting minister	1	0
Police	3	0

The Cambridge Borough election of 1845

The pollbook is in the Guildhall Library.

Result: Fitzroy Kelly, Conservative   746
Shafto Adair, Liberal   729

Selected categories	Adair	Kelly
Solicitors	9	14
Surgeons	6	7
Farmers	3	7
Butchers	3	23
Grocers	26	17
Labourers	5	12
College servants	10	66
Servants	14	41
Publicans	48	29
Gentlemen	47	33
Clergy	4	7
Shoemakers	29	30
Dissenting ministers	5	0
Organists	1	2
Parish clerks	0	2
Turnkey	0	1
Machine maker	0	1
Ironfounders	3	1
Sheriff's officer	0	1
Relieving officers	1	1

The Cambridge Borough election of 1857

The pollbook is in the Guildhall Library.

Result: K. Macaulay, Conservative 769
A. Steuart, Conservative 735
Shafto Adair, Liberal 729
John Hibbert, Liberal 702

Selected categories	Adair	Hibbert	Macaulay	Steuart
Solicitors	9	8	15	16
Surgeons	5	5	11	11
Farmers	2	0	8	7
Butchers	4	3	19	16
Grocers	25	23	17	16
Railwaymen	1	1	1	1
Labourers	3	3	8	7
Servants	16	17	27	25
College servants	11	7	55	48
Publicans	25	27	33	32
Gentlemen	42	38	51	48
Clergy	6	6	11	10
Shoemakers	28	28	24	25
Dissenting ministers	2	2	0	0
Lodging-house keepers	0	0	5	5
Relieving officers	1	1	1	1
Serjeant at mace	1	1	0	0
Sexton	0	0	1	1

The Cambridge Borough election of 1859

The pollbook is in the Guildhall Library.

Result: K. Macaulay, Conservative 752
A. Steuart, Conservative 748
F. Mowatt, Liberal 669
Hon. E. T. Twistleton, Liberal 682

Selected categories	Mowatt	Twistleton	Macaulay	Steuart
Surgeons	5	7	11	11
Farmers	2	2	10	10
Butchers	7	7	15	13
Grocers	21	21	20	20
Labourers	4	4	5	5
Railwaymen	2	2	4	4
Clergymen	2	3	12	12
Shoemakers	25	25	16	17
Dissenting ministers	2	2	0	0
Organists	0	0	3	3
Professors	0	0	3	3
Engineers	2	2	0	0

The Cambridge Borough election of 1859 (cont.)

Selected categories	Mowatt	Twistleton	Macaulay	Steuart
Sheriff's officer	0	0	1	1
Serjeant at mace	1	1	0	0
R.C. priest	1	1	0	0
Parish clerks	0	0	2	2
Editor of *Cambridge Chronicle*	0	0	1	1
Lodginghouse keepers	0	0	2	2

The Cambridge Borough election of 1863

The pollbook is in the Guildhall Library.

Result: Powell, Conservative 708
Fawcett, Liberal 627

Selected categories	Fawcett	Powell
Surgeons	6	13
Farmers	0	5
Butchers	4	13
Grocers	21	12
Labourers	3	3
Railwaymen	0	2
Clergy	2	8
Shoemakers	21	21
Saddlers	1	4
Robemakers	9	6
Gasmen	2	0
Organists	0	3
Tobacco manufacturer	1	0
Engineers	2	0
University marshal	0	1
Lodging-house keepers	1	4
Serjeant at mace	1	0
Registrar	1	0
Sheriff's officer	0	1
Commercial travellers	3	0
Parish clerk	0	1
Professors	0	2
Curator	0	1
Librarians	1	1

The Cambridge Borough election of 1865

The pollbook is in the Guildhall Library.

Result: Forsyth, Conservative   762
Powell, Conservative   760
Torrens, Liberal   726
Christie, Liberal   725

Selected categories	Torrens	Christie	Forsyth	Powell
Solicitors	8	8	15	15
Surgeons	4	5	15	14
Farmers	1	1	6	5
Butchers	7	8	11	13
Grocers	34	31	13	13
Railwaymen	2	2	6	6
Labourers	6	7	1	1
Servants	14	14	24	25
College servants	17	17	70	74
Publicans	41	40	39	39
Clergymen	4	4	20	19
Dissenting ministers	2	3	0	0
Shoemakers	23	23	20	20
Organists	0	0	3	3
Tobacco manufacturer	1	1	0	0
Librarians	2	2	0	0
Relieving officers	2	2	0	0
Parish clerks	0	0	2	2
Cricketers	0	0	3	3
Professors	0	0	4	5
Gaoler	0	0	1	1
Curators	0	0	2	2
Ironfounder	1	1	0	0
Chimney sweeps	0	0	2	3
Lodging-house keepers	0	0	3	3
R.C. priest	1	1	0	0
Town crier	1	1	0	0
Engineers	2	2	0	0

The Cambridge Borough election of 1866

The pollbook is in Cambridge University Library.

Result: John Eldon Gorst, Conservative   774
Lt.-Col. R. R. Torrens, Liberal   755

Virtually all voters are shown below.

		Torrens	Gorst		Torrens	Gorst
I.	Gentlemen	37	61	Agents	5	2
	Farmers	2	6	Military	0	2
II.	Medical	3	19	Officials	13	4
	Legal	7	16	Clerks	26	28

The Cambridge Borough election of 1866 (cont.)

		Torrens	Gorst			Torrens	Gorst
	Teachers	4	4		Booksellers	10	18
	Clergy	7	25		Hairdressers	3	6
	Musicians	4	10		Milkmen	6	10
	Librarians	2	1		Jewellers	1	1
	Organists	0	2		Bakers	38	20
	Miscellaneous	13	22		Hardware	10	5
	professions				Chemists	8	9
					Butchers	9	21
III.	Publicans	30	38		Fruiterers	8	6
IV.	Servants	14	37		Tobacconists	8	2
	College	23	76	VII.	Building	31	29
	servants				craftsmen		
	Railway	1	6		Metalworkers	35	31
	employees				Shoemakers	36	35
	Labourers	5	7		Tailors	71	30
V.	Brewers	19	6		Furniture	22	15
	Builders	21	18		makers		
	Bankers	2	3		Painters	4	7
	Millers	13	5		Printers	25	11
	Maltsters	2	1		Luxury	3	8
	Small manu-	4	1		craftsmen		
	facturers				Leather	9	2
	Coal mer-	3	2		workers		
	chants				Coach	10	4
	Merchants	17	13		builders		
	Hoteliers	0	4		Hatters	1	4
VI.	Grocers	43	21		Sweeps	0	2
	Drapers	45	12		Bookbinders	3	8
	Wine	10	8		Other	9	5
	Fish-	9	2		craftsmen		
	mongers			VIII.	Miscellaneous	10	28

	Summary:	Liberal	Conservative
I.	Gentlemen and farmers	39	67
II.	Professions	84	135
III.	Publicans	30	38
IV.	Labour	43	126
V.	Business	81	53
VI.	Retailers	208	141
VII.	Craftsmen	259	191
VIII.	Miscellaneous	10	28

The Cambridge Borough election of 1868

The pollbook is in Cambridge University Library.

Result: Col. R. R. Torrens, Liberal 1,879
W. Fowler, Liberal 1,857
F. S. Powell, Conservative 1,436
John E. Gorst, Conservative 1,389

The votes analysed were those which were cast for two Liberals or two Tories. Cross voting, or plumping for a single candidate, was omitted from the analysis. The figures therefore are not quite complete, for the totals of split votes were 1,843 in the case of Liberals (out of total votes of 1,879 and 1,857 for their men) and 1,382 for the Tories (out of total polls of 1,436 and 1,389).

All voters	Liberal	Con-servative			Liberal	Con-servative
I. Gentlemen	61	78	VI. Craftsmen and skilled workers			
Farmers	3	13	Leather		13	5
			Luxury		12	9
II. Professional and commercial			Hatters		2	7
Legal	10	19	Painters		45	29
Medical	7	22	Furniture		42	25
Clergy	13	34	Printers		46	17
Officials	12	10	Tailors		176	51
Musicians	5	8	Shoemakers		121	63
Organists	0	5	Metal		118	62
Teachers	8	12	Building		207	85
Librarians	2	4	craftsmen			
Military	0	4	Coach-		12	9
Agents and Brokers	7	6	builders			
Clerks	54	39	Bookbinders		8	10
Miscellaneous	13	32	Minor crafts		7	14
			Sweeps		0	7
III. Publicans	41	40	VII. Retailers			
IV. Labour			Wine		10	7
Labourers	214	108	Fish		5	4
Railwaymen	75	15	Tobacco		4	3
Servants	65	120	Milk		10	16
College servants	25	115	Hardware		23	11
			Chemists		7	11
V. Business			Bakers		44	28
Hoteliers	0	2	Booksellers		9	19
Brewers	18	16	Green-grocers		8	7
Builders	24	23	Jewellers		7	1
Maltsters	9	1	Drapers		51	14
Millers	23	3	Grocers		53	22
Coal merchants	9	5	Hairdressers		4	7
Merchants	36	19	Butchers		12	32
Bankers	2	1	VIII. Miscellaneous	39	57	
Small manufacturers	8	2				

The Cambridge Borough election of 1868 (cont.)

'Miscellaneous' included the following. Tories: lamplighter, students, 9 cricketers, carter, cabman, stablekeeper, undertaker, pianotuner, billiards-keeper, artist, photographer, lodging-house keeper, sexton, moneylender, hawker, eating-house keeper. Liberals: pieman, drover, cattledealer, money-lender, carter, pianotuner, chiropodist, horsekeeper, eating-house and lodging-house keepers, watermen, ten firemen and seven hawkers, artist, photographer. All the hoteliers, organists, cricketers, students, lamplighters, billiards-keepers, sweeps, and military men were Tories. All the firemen and Dissenting clergy were Liberal.

Summary:		Liberal	Conservative
I.	Gentlemen and farmers	64	91
II.	Professional and commercial	131	195
III.	Publicans	41	40
IV.	Labour	379	359
V.	Business	129	72
VI.	Craftsmen and skilled workers	809	393
VII.	Retailers	247	182
VIII.	Miscellaneous	39	57

The Cambridge Borough Election of 1868

Tenders

The Cambridge pollbook for 1868 in the Guildhall Library has an appendix listing votes tendered by members of the University, etc., pending a legal decision. 'The right of members of the University to vote as lodgers under the Representation of the People Act, 1867, being at the time of the Election the subject of an appeal in the Court of Common Pleas, the following Members of the University tendered their votes, pending the decision of the Court.'

	Torrens (Liberal)	Fowler (Liberal)	Powell (Conservative)	Gorst (Conservative)
Students	3	3	34	35
Clerks in holy orders	0	0	3	3
Scholars	0	0	3	3
Fellows	0	0	9	9
Lecturers	0	0	1	1
Gentlemen	0	0	1	1
Barrister	1	1	0	0

The Cambridge University election of 1831

The Times for 9 May 1831 contains on page 3 this item, which is reproduced as it stands:

'One of the weekly papers maintains that the electors of Cambridge "come from no particular class, and are of no particular professions". An examination of the pollbook will soon dissipate this error...The numbers subjoined are not given as altogether accurate, but may be relied on within a few, and show pretty

The Cambridge University election of 1831 (cont.)

plainly in what "particular class and professions" Messrs. Goulburn and Peel have found their majorities.

	Clergy	Laity	Total
Goulburn	570	236	806
Peel	573	232	805
Cavendish	323	307	630
Palmerston	309	301	610'

According to *The Times* for 19 May 1831, the professors of the University of Cambridge were distinctly for Reform. Fifteen voted for Palmerston and Cavendish, and only 6 for Goulburn and Peel.

The Carlisle elections of 1865 and 1868

The following electors in Carlisle were employed by the London and North Western Railway:

In 1865 30:   of whom 27 voted Tory.
In 1868 154:   of whom 136 voted Tory.

The following voters were employees of the North Eastern Railway:

In 1868 45:   of whom 27 voted Liberal;
of whom 8 voted Tory.

The Tory candidate for Carlisle was a director of the London and North Western Railway; the chairman of the North Eastern line had been a Liberal M.P. for Whitby.

Sources: *Parl. Papers 1868–9*, VIII, 367–8, qq. 9359, 9393, 9398.

The Chatham election of 1857

The pollbook is in the Guildhall Library.

Result: Col. Sir Frederick Smith, Conservative   672
W. G. Romaine, Liberal   643

Selected categories	Romaine	Smith
Anglican clergy	0	6
Dissenting ministers	3	0
Bankers	0	2
Farmers	4	7
Policemen	4	4
Pensioners	5	7
Brewers	0	4
Victuallers	38	58
Tailors	19	13
Shoemakers	25	18
Grocers	29	18
Butchers	13	20
Carpenters	11	16
Mariners	12	1
Sailmakers	3	2
Gentlemen	45	45
Army, Navy, Marines	16	15
Shipwrights	31	39
Dockyard	82	104

The Chatham election of 1859

The pollbook is in the Guildhall Library. For about 50 voters, no occupation was stated.

Result: Maj.-Gen. Sir F. Smith, Conservative   713
A. J. Otway, Liberal   652

Selected categories	Otway	Smith
Anglican clergy	0	6
Dissenting ministers	1	0
Bankers	2	2
Farmers	3	6
Policemen	5	2
Pensioners	6	9
Brewers	0	3
Victuallers	41	56
Beersellers	0	3
Tailors	19	14
Shoemakers	19	14
Grocers	28	20
Butchers	14	19
Carpenters	13	15
Mariners	10	4
Sailmakers	3	3
Gentlemen	45	33
Army, Navy, Marines	16	19
Shipwrights	35	31
Dockyard	85	119

The Chester election of 1859

The pollbook is in Chester Public Library.

Result: Earl Grosvenor, Liberal   1,464
Humberston, Liberal-Conservative   1,110
Salisbury, Radical   708

Breakdown of the 708 Radical voters

A. £10 householders

'Householders'	133
Publicans	15
Shopkeepers	79
Craftsmen	13
Brewers, ironfounders, farmer, dealers	8
Doctor, teacher, solicitors	4
	252

B. Freemen voters

I. Shopkeepers 33
Bakers 19

II. Shoemakers 35
Tailors 24
Building craftsmen 48

Wood workers	62
Metal workers	36
Printers	15
Leather workers	14
Other craftsmen	47

III. Gentlemen 6
Brewer, builders, shipbuilder, ironfounders, hop merchant, coachmakers 17
Architect, auctioneer, accountant 3

IV. Clerks 16
Labourers 40
Others 41

The Chester election of 1859 (cont.)

Summary of the Radical vote

£10 householders		252
Freemen		
I.	Retailers	52
II.	Craftsmen	281
III.	Upper crust	26
IV.	Miscellaneous	97
		708

The Chichester election of 2–4 August 1830

The pollbook is in the Guildhall Library.

Result: Lord George Lennox   643
John Smith   527
C. Sinclair Cullen   219

Smith and Cullen both claimed to be for Reform and for Civil and Religious Liberty. Cullen was an Anglican, and pledged himself to support any measure of reform, however sweeping, to reduce taxation, and to abolish negro slavery. Lennox had no platform, but claimed to be independent of all parties. According to *Dod*, however, Lennox supported the Reform Bills and generally acted with the Whigs for several years, before returning to the Tories.

Selected categories	Lennox	Cullen	Smith
Clergymen	11	0	7
Chorister	1	0	1
Organist	1	0	1
Vergers	3	0	3
Unitarian minister	0	1	0
Freemen	28	1	9
Corporators	18	0	12
Drapers	9	3	7
Butchers	18	10	13
Grocers	19	14	16
Publicans	23	3	21
Labourers	41	10	50
Carpenters	24	14	15
Woolsorters	5	1	3
Gentlemen	43	10	31
Tailors	20	7	17
Shoemakers	29	13	29
Surgeons	9	1	7
Bankers	6	0	5

The Chichester election of 2–3 May 1831

The pollbook is in the Guildhall Library.

Result: Lord Arthur Lennox   665
John Abel Smith   388
Sir Godfrey Webster, Bt.   306

Selected categories	Lennox	Webster	Smith
Clergymen	8	0	6
Organist	1	0	1
Precentor	1	0	1
Verger	1	0	1
Unitarian minister	1	1	0
Freemen	12	4	8
Corporators	16	1	12
Drapers	12	4	9
Butchers	22	12	9
Grocers	23	13	12
Publicans	21	7	14
Labourers	46	27	30
Carpenters	30	23	11
Gentlemen	52	12	41
Shoemakers	36	20	19
Surgeons	8	0	6
Tailors	24	14	10
Bankers	3	1	1

The Colchester election of 30 March 1831

The pollbook is in the Guildhall Library.

Result: William Mayhew, Whig   604
Sir Wm. Curtis, Tory   490

Resident voters only

Selected categories	Curtis	Mayhew
Aldermen	7	1
Common Councilmen	12	0
Gentlemen	10	6
Farmers	4	1
Cordwainers	15	24
Labourers	23	14
Weavers	2	0
Ironfounders	0	4
Serjeants at mace	3	0
Town crier	1	0
Parish clerk	1	0
Mayor	1	0
Silk weavers	1	5
Tinplate worker	0	1

Voters resident outside Colchester

Selected categories	Curtis	Mayhew
Weavers and silk weavers	13	21
Silk manufacturers	0	1

The Dover election of July–August 1830

The pollbook is in the Institute of Historical Research.

Result: C. Poulett Thompson, Reformer — 992
Sir John Rae Reid, Tory — 986
John Halcomb, Tory — 748

Reid had the interest of the Lord Warden. Halcomb was a Tory barrister and the son of a coach proprietor, and stood for Dover as an Anti-Catholic candidate.

The figures in the first table are based on an analysis of the whole pollbook for the categories concerned. The figures in the second are based on an analysis of about half the pollbook.

Selected categories	Thompson	Reid	Halcomb
Officers	6	13	1
Sextons	2	2	0
Surgeon	7	10	1
Pilots	41	62	18
Dissenting ministers	1	0	2
Butchers	10	18	26
Grocers	23	13	24

Selected categories	Thompson	Reid	Halcomb
Gentlemen	36	42	22
Victuallers	18	13	20
Carpenters	25	28	23
Cordwainers	25	14	22
Tailors	23	20	12
Mariners	42	41	38
Labourers	18	23	22

The Dover election of December 1832

The pollbook is in the Institute of Historical Research.

Result: C. P. Thompson, Liberal — 713
Sir J. R. Reid, Conservative — 644
John Halcomb, Conservative — 523
Capt. Stanhope, R.N., Liberal — 498

Freemen only:

selected categories	Thompson	Stanhope	Reid	Halcomb
Officers	3	2	3	0
Surgeons	1	1	5	1
Dissenting minister	1	1	0	0
Parish clerks	0	0	2	0
Sexton	1	0	1	0
Pilots	11	3	33	12
Grocers	12	11	8	13
Butchers	8	5	11	23

Plumps		Splits	
Thompson	28	Thompson and Reid	173
Reid	200	Thompson and Halcomb	53
Halcomb	191	Thompson and Stanhope	459
Stanhope	5	Reid and Halcomb	258
		Reid and Stanhope	13
		Halcomb and Stanhope	21

The Dover by-election of 1833

The pollbook is in the Institute of Historical Research.

Result: John Halcomb, Conservative   734
         Capt. Stanhope, R.N., Liberal   665

Freemen only:

selected categories	Stanhope	Halcomb
Gentlemen	46	46
Clergymen	0	1
Sexton	1	0
Parish clerks	0	2
Surgeons	1	5
Policemen	1	1
Officers	2	2
Dissenting minister	1	0
Innkeepers	23	42
Pilots	9	29
Tailors	33	24
Carpenters	29	24
Butchers	5	24
Grocers	15	17
Mariners	54	58
Cordwainers	26	26

The Dover election of 1835

The pollbook is in the Institute of Historical Research.

Result: J. M. Fector, Conservative   908 (a Dover man)
        Sir J. R. Reid, Conservative   782
        E. R. Rice, Liberal   761

Freemen only:

selected categories	Rice	Fector	Reid
Anglican clergyman	0	0	1
Sexton	0	1	1
Parish clerks	0	2	2
Officers	1	4	3
Surgeons	0	5	5
Dissenting ministers	1	1	0
Innkeepers	27	43	36
Butchers	11	19	19
Grocers	20	21	17
Pilots	8	15	39

Plumps		Splits	
Fector	25	Fector and Reid	549
Reid	110	Fector and Rice	336
Rice	302	Reid and Rice	126

The Dover election of 1837

The pollbook is in the Institute of Historical Research.

Result: E. R. Rice, Liberal 854
Sir J. R. Reid, Conservative 829
J. M. Fector, Conservative 742

Freemen only:

selected categories	Rice	Reid	Fector
Pilots	8	36	28
Policemen	3	10	9
Parish clerks	0	2	2
Surgeons	0	5	5
Solicitors	0	3	3
Dissenting minister	1	0	0
Harbour master	0	1	0
Sexton	1	1	0
Anglican clergyman	0	1	1
Gaoler	0	1	1
Officers	0	2	2
Butchers	10	19	14
Grocers	24	11	15
Cordwainers	29	24	15
Mariners	61	49	32
Labourers	36	36	26

Plumps		Splits	
Rice	536	Rice and Reid	194
Reid	39	Rice and Fector	126
Fector	20	Reid and Fector	596

Polled		Unpolled	
Freemen	1,060	Freemen	102
£10 Electors	451	£10 Electors	64
	1,511		

The Dublin City elections of 1857, 1859 and 1865

The candidates in the elections of 1857 and 1859 were:

	1857	1859
Grogan (G), Conservative	3,767	4,251
Vance (V), Conservative	3,711	4,224
Brady (B), Liberal	3,405	3,976
Reynolds (R), Liberal	3,348	—
McCarthy (McC), Liberal	—	3,881

The candidates in 1865 were:

Guinness (G), Conservative	4,739
Pim (P), Liberal	4,653
Vance (V), Conservative	4,073

The Dublin City elections of 1857, 1859 and 1865 (cont.)

I. The voting of builders

There were 43 builders on the register altogether. These voted as follows:

No. of builders	1857	1859	1865
18	G V	G V	G V
5	R B	B McC	P
2	—	—	P
4	—	—	G V
3	R B	B McC	G P
2	—	—	G P
2	—	—	V
1	G V	G V	—
3	—	G V	G V
1	G V	—	G P
1	—	—	V P
1	G B	G V	G V
43			

II. The voting of particular surnames

DONNELLY: 13 of these voted: of whom 11 voted some form of: R B, B McC, P.

MURPHY: There were 92 Murphys voting. Almost without exception they voted some form of R B, B McC, P.

WHELAN: There were 16 Whelans voting.

	1857	1859	1865
14	R B	B McC	P
1	B	B McC	G P
1	—	—	V G

M'EVOY:	1857	1859	1865
7	R B	B McC	P
2	—	B McC	P
1	—	B McC	—

M'GRATH:	1857	1859	1865
5	R B	B McC	P
1	R B	B McC	—

DUNNE: 54 Dunnes are given. In 11 cases, occupations are stated: these all voted some combination of G V, G V, G V. Of the 43 whose occupation is not given, 29 are some combinations of R B, B McC, P. There were 6 Patrick Dunnes, all voting some form of R B, B McC, P.

H

The Dublin City elections of 1857, 1859 and 1865 (cont.)

III. The pollbook being very large, only certain sections of it were transcribed and sent to me. The analysis below is of about 2,500 voters whose names began with M, Mc, Mac, M', O and O', C and D, and A and part of B.

	1857				1859				1865		
	G	V	R	B	G	V	B	McC	G	V	P
Rev. Dr Cullen	o	o	1	1	o	o	o	o	o	o	1
Clergymen	25	25	2	2	34	34	5	5	36	34	12
Gentlemen	66	63	11	13	73	73	12	12	98	96	20
Surgeons	17	17	5	8	17	17	5	5	26	22	11
Lawyers	45	44	6	8	65	64	12	10	60	63	14
Minor professions	12	11	1	1	15	15	2	2	28	28	2
Merchants	17	17	7	7	22	22	7	7	16	22	12
Clerks	6	6	o	o	11	11	o	o	26	30	3
Yeomen	12	12	1	1	15	14	3	2	13	15	4
Druggists	6	6	o	o	7	7	o	o	7	8	1
Grocers, chandlers	11	11	5	5	14	14	8	7	19	15	12
Drapers, hosiers	8	8	o	o	10	10	o	o	6	9	o
Jewellers, etc.	7	7	2	3	5	5	4	4	7	6	4
Brassfounders	7	7	1	1	8	8	3	3	10	11	6
Housepainters	6	6	1	1	6	6	o	o	9	9	1
Furniture workers	11	11	6	6	12	12	6	6	16	17	7
Printers	19	19	2	2	21	22	5	4	21	23	8
Weavers, tailors	10	9	3	2	11	10	2	1	12	11	6
Tanners	3	3	o	o	3	3	o	o	3	3	o
Plumbers	3	3	o	o	3	3	o	o	6	6	1
Shoemakers	9	9	1	1	6	6	2	2	10	10	2
General unskilled	12	12	27	26	12	13	27	26	19	17	39

The Durham City election of 1832

The pollbook is in the Guildhall Library.

Result: W. C. Harland, Liberal   439
W. R. C. Chaytor, Liberal   403
Hon. A. Trevor, Conservative   383

Freemen and householders: selected categories	Harland	Chaytor	Trevor
Anglican clergy	5	3	15
Verger	o	o	1
Organist	o	o	1
Choristers	o	o	2
Dissenting minister	1	1	o
Mayor of Durham	1	1	o
Town clerk of Durham	1	1	o
Pitmen	2	2	5

The Durham City by-election of 1843

The pollbook is in the Institute of Historical Research.

Result:

	John Bright, Liberal	Thos. Purvis, Conservative
Freemen	284	230
£10 Householders	204	180
	488	410

For all the householders, and for about one-fifth of the freemen voters, no particulars of occupations were given. All the other freemen voters appear in the table below:

Selected categories	Bright	Purvis
Surgeon	0	1
Solicitors	2	0
Innkeeper	1	0
Butchers	8	5
Grocers	2	0
Drapers	2	6
Shoemakers	28	22
Leather crafts	18	10
Painters	6	8
Tailors	29	10
Masons	25	22
Plumbers	7	6
Ropers	9	2
Smiths	8	3
Weavers	4	0
Wood workers	33	26
Pitmen	4	1
Labourers	3	3
Others	15	11

The Anglican clergy voted as ten-pound householders as follows:

	Bright	Purvis	Abstained
Anglican clergy	1	13	6

The Durham (North) election of 1868

The pollbook is in Cambridge University Library.

Result: G. Elliot, Conservative	4,649
Sir H. Williamson, Liberal	4,011
I. L. Bell, Liberal	3,822

Voting of clergy

For Williamson	20
For Bell	19
For Elliot	68
Abstained	9

The Durham (South) election of 1868

The pollbook is in Cambridge University Library.

Result: J. W. Pease, Liberal   4,321
       F. E. B. Beaumont, Liberal   4,021
       C. F. Surtees, Conservative   3,726
       Hon. G. R. Hamilton-Russell,
         Conservative   3,215

Voting of clergy
  For Pease   6
  For Beaumont   5
  For Surtees   84
  For Russell   84
  Abstained   26 (mostly living outside the county)

The Edinburgh election of 1852

The pollbook is in the Guildhall Library.

Result: Macaulay, Liberal   1,872
       Cowan, Liberal   1,754
       Provost Maclaren, Liberal   1,559
       Bruce, Conservative   1,066
       Campbell, Liberal-Conservative   626

Selected categories	Macaulay	Cowan	Provost Maclaren	Campbell	Bruce
Manufacturers	4	3	4	1	0
Merchants	59	73	42	27	29
Surgeons	35	29	11	9	13
Writers	40	33	8	5	29
Shoemakers	37	33	46	15	14
Grocers	60	58	56	19	19
Clergy and ministers	6	16	13	9	11
Bankers	4	14	1	9	11
Police	2	1	1	0	1
Railwaymen	1	1	0	0	0

The Essex (East) election of 1868

The pollbook is in the Guildhall Library. It does not give occupations, but clergymen can be identified by their prefix.

Result: James Round, Conservative   2,861
       S. B. Ruggles-Brise, Conservative   2,816
       Sir T. B. Western, Liberal   2,224
       Sir T. N. Abdy, Liberal   2,134

	Western	Abdy	Round	Brise
Clergy	12	12	176	177

The Exeter election of April 1831

The pollbook is in the Guildhall Library.

Result: Wentworth Buller, Whig   753
        Buck, Tory   548
        Divett, Whig   379

Resident voters only:*
selected categories

	Buller	Buck	Divett
Gentlemen	37	30	17
Shoemakers	15	10	9
Weaver	1	0	1
Labourers	3	3	3
Clergy	7	13	3
Vergers	0	3	0
Lay vicars	2	2	0
Surgeons	7	9	0
Fullers	32	26	11
Wool and worsted manufacturers	3	4	1
Parish clerks	2	3	0
Town crier	1	1	0
Aldermen	3	3	0
Serjeants at mace	1	3	0
Governor of workhouse	1	1	0
Sheriff's officers	2	2	0
Dissenting minister	1	0	1
Fringe manufacturer	1	1	0
Starch manufacturer	1	1	0

* This excludes out-voters.

The Glasgow election of 1832

The pollbook is in Manchester Public Library.

Result: James Ewing   3,214
        James Oswald   2,838
        Sir D. K. Sandford 2,168
        John Crawfurd   1,850
        John Douglas   1,340
        Joseph Dixon   995

Selected categories

	Ewing	Oswald	Sandford	Crawfurd	Dixon	Douglas
Ministers*	28	7	6	7	2	6
Surgeons	57	47	48	43	13	33
Manufacturers	203	158	99	80	41	24
Merchants	474	310	144	126	131	46
Cotton merchants	13	17	2	5	1	0
Cotton spinners	13	13	0	2	0	1

* The Rev. Dr Ralph Wardlaw plumped for Ewing. The R.C. bishop voted for Ewing and Oswald.

The Glasgow election of 1832 (cont.)

Selected categories	Ewing	Oswald	Sandford	Crawfurd	Dixon	Douglas
Weavers	23	28	81	39	16	65
Brewers	9	6	8	2	4	5
Victuallers	38	46	47	37	23	25
Grocers	105	114	140	95	41	79
Shoemakers	48	41	51	40	16	32
Farmers	12	15	1	5	1	2

The *Annual Register* commented on this election: 'In Glasgow...a strong but unsuccessful battle was fought for Radicalism. It selected for its members an accomplished and moderate-minded merchant, and gave him for his colleague a practised Whig.'

The Grantham election of 1865

The pollbook is in the Bodleian Library.

Result: Thorold, Conservative 432
Welby, Conservative 404
Tollemache, Liberal 315

Selected categories	Tollemache	Thorold	Welby
Grocers	13	12	11
Butchers	17	10	12
Shoemakers	16	8	6
Surgeons	4	6	7
Farmers	12	33	32
Railwaymen	0	3	3
Organist	1	0	0
R.C. priest	1	0	0
Clergymen	1	5	6
Sexton	0	1	1
Wesleyan minister	0	1	1

The Halifax election of 1847

The pollbook is in Manchester Public Library.

Result: Henry Edwards, Conservative 511
Sir C. Wood, Whig 507
E. Miall, Radical 351
E. Jones, Chartist 280

I. Drink

	Jones	Miall	Wood	Edwards
Spirit merchants	0	1	7	7
Publicans	8	7	27	30
Brewer	0	0	0	1
Beersellers	3	3	6	8
Coopers	0	0	2	2

The Halifax election of 1847 (cont.)

II. Upper crust and dependants

	Jones	Miall	Wood	Edwards
Gentlemen	1	2	9	13
Solicitors	1	1	10	13
Doctors	1	1	11	12
Clergy	3	3	4	4
Architects	0	0	2	2
Surveyors	0	0	4	4
Schoolmasters	2	3	1	2
Clerks	0	1	3	3
Farmers	2	1	3	4
Sexton	0	0	1	1
Gardeners	0	0	1	3
Other respectables*	5	7	24	26

* Registrar, dentist, relieving officer, accountant, artists, inspector, bank manager, vet., insurance agents, stockbrokers, bailiffs, auctioneers, music teachers, designers, opticians.

III. Textiles, all classes

	Jones	Miall	Wood	Edwards
Cardmakers	4	8	12	8
Dyers	7	6	7	7
Manufacturers	7	15	22	15
Woolstaplers	2	8	19	13
Carpet weaver	1	1	0	0
Cloth dresser	0	0	1	0
Worsted spinners	1	2	2	1

IV. Business, except textiles

	Jones	Miall	Wood	Edwards
Organbuilders	0	0	2	2
Coachmakers	0	0	2	2
Corn millers and dealers	7	7	10	8
Ironfounders	0	0	5	5
Merchants	1	1	8	8
Others	2	4	7	4

V. Crafts

	Jones	Miall	Wood	Edwards
Watchmakers	2	1	6	3
Light metal crafts	7	9	7	3
Leather	6	11	11	7
Building trades	4	5	3	5
Blacksmiths	2	2	1	1
Machine makers	6	6	3	2
Cloggers	6	4	2	2
Tailors	10	8	6	4
Shoemakers	4	6	9	7

The Halifax election of 1847 (cont.)

V. Crafts (*cont.*)

	Jones	Miall	Wood	Edwards
Woodworkers	5	9	11	11
Printers	3	3	2	2
Plumbers	2	2	2	4
Others*	4	9	2	6

* Cork, basket, button, rope trades, carver, gilder.

VI. Shopkeepers

	Jones	Miall	Wood	Edwards
Grocers and general	37	37	22	19
Hatters	3	3	2	2
Booksellers	3	3	5	5
Drapers	14	17	9	7
Tobacconists	1	1	2	2
Butchers	1	1	6	7
Hairdressers	6	5	5	3
Furniture	2	3	1	0
Milkman	1	1	0	0
Druggists	3	2	6	5
Clothes brokers	3	3	1	2
Ironmongers	3	4	3	2
Pawnbrokers	2	2	1	1

VII. Unclassified*

Jones	Miall	Wood	Edwards
78	102	158	180

Summary:	Jones	Miall	Wood	Edwards
I. Drink	11	11	42	48
II. Upper crust	10	12	48	61
III. Textiles	22	40	63	44
IV. Other business	10	12	34	29
V. Crafts	59	75	65	57
VI. Shopkeepers	79	82	63	55
VII. Unclassified	78	102	158	180

* I.e. occupations not stated in the pollbook.

Reg. no. of Electors		1,022
Edwards:	plumps	108
	and Wood	370
	and Miall	19
	and Jones	14
Wood:	plumps	60
	and Edwards	370
	and Miall	59
	and Jones	14
Miall:	plumps	26
	and Jones	245
Jones:	plumps	3
	and Miall	245

The Hereford City election of 1826

The pollbook is in the Institute of Historical Research.

Result: The Rt. Hon. John Somers, Viscount Eastnor, Tory 667
      E. B. Clive, Whig   453
      R. Blakemore, Tory   437

Selected categories	Clive	Eastnor	Blakemore
Gentlemen	73	129	75
Clergymen	13	35	25
Officers	5	11	5
Surgeons	3	6	4
Victuallers	33	42	31
Farmers	31	29	14
Tailors	26	33	19
Shoemakers	25	36	27
Grocers	12	15	4
Butchers	9	16	11
Weavers	2	8	6
Labourers	26	36	25

The Hereford City election of 1832

The pollbook is in the Institute of Historical Research.

Result: E. B. Clive, Liberal   392
      Robert Biddulph, Liberal   380
      R. Blakemore, Conservative 245

Freemen and £10 householders:

selected categories	Clive	Biddulph	Blakemore
Gentlemen	38	37	19
Clergymen	6	6	14
Officers	2	2	2
Surgeons	2	2	1
Farmers	16	17	3
Victuallers	16	12	17
Beersellers	1	2	0
Grocers	26	27	4
Butchers	12	11	9
Tailors	21	21	15
Shoemakers	13	14	15
Lawyers	5	6	6
Weavers	1	1	2
Labourers	14	13	21
Dissenting minister	1	1	0
Verger	0	0	1
Sexton	0	0	1

The Hereford City election of 1835

The pollbook is in the Institute of Historical Research.

Result: E. B. Clive, Liberal   457   Plumps: 4
   Robt. Biddulph, Liberal   435   3
   R. Blakemore, Conservative 426   301

Freemen voters:

selected categories	Clive	Biddulph	Blakemore
Gentlemen	30	23	23
Clergymen	9	8	19
Officers	3	3	5
Surgeon	0	0	1
Solicitors	12	9	11
Farmers	12	11	8
Grocers	9	9	2
Butchers	6	5	8
Tailors	12	11	13
Victuallers	11	12	28
Weavers	0	0	4
Labourers	8	8	8

£10 householders:

selected categories	Clive	Biddulph	Blakemore
Gentlemen	20	21	7
Clergymen*	7	6	7
Officers	2	1	2
Surgeons	7	6	1
Solicitors	6	6	3
Bankers	1	1	0
Farmers	18	15	7
Grocers	15	16	4
Butchers	5	7	9
Tailors	14	8	10
Victuallers	4	5	9
Labourers	3	4	4
Verger	0	0	1
Dissenting ministers	2	2	0

* The Dean of Hereford voted for Blakemore.

The Herefordshire election of 1868

The pollbook is in the Guildhall Library. It does not give occupations.

Result: Sir H. Croft, Conservative   3,351
   Sir J. R. Bailey, Conservative   3,341
   M. Biddulph, Liberal   2,273
   Thomas Blake, Liberal   1,878

	Biddulph	Blake	Croft	Bailey
Clergy	15	7	61	61

The Hertfordshire election of December 1832

The pollbook is in the Guildhall Library. It does not state occupations.

Result: Sir J. S. Sebright, Bart, Liberal   2,154
N. Calvert, Liberal   2,141
Viscount Grimston, Conservative   2,074
R. Alston, Liberal   2,007

	Sebright	Calvert	Alston	Grimston
Clergy	25	27	20	64

The Huddersfield election of 1834

The pollbook is in Huddersfield Public Library.

Result: John Blackburne, K.C., Liberal 234
Michael T. Sadler, Conservative 147
Capt. Joseph Wood, Liberal 108

All voters	Wood	Blackburne	Sadler
Merchants and manufacturers	10	44	20
Woolstaplers	0	11	16
Cloth drawers	0	4	0
Cloth dressers	0	15	8
Innkeepers and beersellers	22	16	5
Farmers	7	8	13
Tailors	5	3	3
Shoemakers	5	0	4
Corn dealers	2	0	3
Butchers	3	2	2
Ironmongers	2	0	3
Leather trades	1	8	1
Maltsters	1	0	5
Grocers	23	14	6
Druggists	0	3	2
Drapers, hatters	10	2	4
Clergy	0	0	3
Attorneys	0	8	5
Surgeons	0	6	2
Yarn dealers	0	5	1
Ironfounders	0	2	0
Dyers	0	7	1
Joiners, painters, masons, plasterers	1	15	4
Plumbers, glaziers	0	4	0
Miscellaneous	17	51	34

The 1834 pollbook contains these remarks:

'Who does Lawyer Blackburne represent? Why, not the men of Huddersfield, under the haggard form of a few dead body-bill doctors, factory-mongers, Mushroom Merchants, and their Myrmidons, who are instinctively against the

The Huddersfield election of 1834 (cont.)

people, as the shark is against the herring...However, that these Sharks of Society may be known, in order to be avoided as much as possible, the following "List of Voters" is published, so that every Patriot may distinguish his Friend from his Enemy.'

'They [£10 voters] have a second time set aside the man of your choice. Yes; and they glory in the deed. If these new Boroughmongers will have the power exclusively, let them enjoy their trade after the same Reforming fashion. Touch their POCKETS, and their spurious INDEPENDENCE will lick the dust...by this you will conquer. Remember, and never forget, that *labour* is the only earthly handmaid of wealth, power, and safety. You, the unrepresented, are the BEES: let the DRONES take care of themselves till they learn to whom the hive belongs...'

The Huddersfield election of 1837

The pollbook is in Huddersfield Public Library.

Result: Edward Ellice, jun., Liberal   340
Richard Oastler, Conservative   290

All voters	Edward Ellice, jun.	Oastler
Merchants and manufacturers	51	24
Banker	0	1
Attorneys	7	6
Surgeons	7	4
Magistrates	0	2
Farmers	7	51
Ironfounders, machine makers	6	0
Sir J. Ramsden's agents	6	0
Innkeepers, etc.	25	38
Spirit merchants	4	4
Grocers	21	20
Corn dealers	2	3
Tailors	7	5
Shoemakers, cloggers	5	11
Drapers, hatters	14	10
Druggists	5	1
Butchers	6	4
Booksellers, stationers	4	4
Masons, painters, joiners, plasterers	19	9
Woolstaplers	13	20
Tinner, brazier, ironmongers	5	6
Hairdressers	1	3
Heald and slay makers	2	2
Cloth dressers and drawers	28	13
Clothes dealers	2	4
Coopers	1	3
Dyers	11	2
Leather crafts	5	0
Clock and watch makers	4	0
Miscellaneous	56	40

The Huddersfield election of 1837 (cont.)

The 1837 pollbook concludes with this message:

'In the above list you may behold your opponents in their true colours:—there are the determined supporters of Bastiles and bad government in all its shapes... Is it for this we have formed an Anti-Poor Law Association? Is it for this we have organized the surrounding Hamlets for the purpose of making every possible resistance to the introduction of the "Starvation Law"?... Thus they despise the poor and send their enemies to Parliament, to make laws for their further oppression... it is neither your duty nor your interest to support them; but directly the reverse. The WAY to their brains is through their pockets —FIND IT.'

The Hull election of 29–30 July 1830

The pollbook is in the Guildhall Library.

Result: G. Schonswar, Tory   1,564
W. B. Wrightson, Whig   1,213
T. G. Burke, Whig   869

Schonswar was an Alderman and former Mayor of Hull, a Justice of the Peace and Deputy Lieutenant for the East Riding.

Voters A–D inclusive only

	Wrightson	Burke	Schonswar
Mariners	23	37	43
Shipwrights	21	32	35

Voters A–Z

Selected categories	Wrightson	Burke	Schonswar
Cordwainers	36	30	45
Officers	2	2	4
Merchants	20	6	57
Butchers	30	29	32
Grocers	10	5	10
Pilots	3	2	11
Shipbuilders	1	0	4
Victuallers	10	6	10
Gaoler	0	0	1
Town clerk	0	0	1
Surgeons	3	0	5
Sexton	0	0	1
Mayor's officers	1	0	3
Shipowners	3	0	2
Police	1	0	1
Beadle	0	0	1
'Commodore of the pilots'	0	0	1

The Huntingdon election of 1832

The pollbook is in the Institute of Historical Research.

Result: Col. F. Peel, Conservative   177
F. Pollock, Conservative   171
Capt. Duberly, Liberal   128
E. Maltby, Liberal   94

Selected categories	Duberly	Peel
Gentlemen	13	17
Doctor	1	0
Solicitors	2	4
Teachers	2	3
Servants	2	16
Surveyor	1	0
Builders	1	1
Brewers	4	2
Merchants*	7	15
Publicans	9	14
Shoemakers	5	12
Tailors†	11	6
Building crafts‡	16	27
Metal crafts§	4	7
Minor crafts**	22	21
Grocers	4	7
Druggist	1	1
Jeweller	1	0
Ironmongers	1	2
Drapers	3	2
Butchers	5	7
Bakers	9	9
Coachmaker	1	0

State of the poll

	Liberal		Conservative	
	Duberly	Maltby	Peel	Pollock
Huntingdon Old Electors (Burgesses)	5	4	61	62
Huntingdon electors newly enfranchised	59	49	73	71
Godmanchester electors	64	41	43	38

* Includes millers, corn factors, wholesalers.
† Includes glovers.
‡ Includes woodworkers and painters.
§ Includes watchmakers.
** Includes cottagers and handymen.

The Ipswich election of 1832

The pollbook is in Manchester University Library.

Result: Morrison, Liberal   594
Wason, Liberal   593
E. Goulburn, Conservative   308
Fitzroy Kelly, Conservative   265
C. Mackinnon, Conservative   94

Selected categories	Morrison	Wason	Goulburn	Kelly	Mackinnon
Gentlemen	45	43	29	25	11
Lawyers	5	5	9	7	5
Physicians	5	5	4	4	0
Dissenting ministers	3	2	0	0	0
Brewers	7	7	0	0	0
Publicans	30	31	10	10	3
Farmers	8	8	16	14	2
Grocers	15	17	11	11	0
Butchers	14	14	5	5	0
Shoemakers	27	27	11	9	1
Shipwrights	4	4	3	3	0
Mariners	29	29	11	10	4

The Ipswich election of 1835

The pollbook is in Manchester University Library.

Result: Morrison, Liberal   542
Wason, Liberal   533
Broke, Conservative   454
Holmes, Conservative   434

New Constituency		Old Constituency	
Morrison	393	Morrison	149
Wason	385	Wason	148
Broke	291	Broke	163
Holmes	274	Holmes	160

Selected categories	Morrison	Wason	Broke	Holmes
Gentlemen	50	50	66	66
Lawyers	3	3	13	10
Physicians	8	6	5	3
Dissenting ministers	3	3	0	0
Brewers	4	4	1	1
Publicans	21	21	21	21
Beersellers	3	3	0	0
Farmers	4	3	19	18
Grocers	17	17	13	11
Butchers	12	12	14	11
Shoemakers	17	17	13	12
Shipwrights	4	4	1	1
Mariners	39	38	21	20
Master mariners	4	4	0	0
Parish clerk	0	0	1	1
Sweep	0	0	1	1

The Ipswich election of 1847

There are two pollbooks covering this election, one in Manchester University Library, the other in the Institute of Historical Research.

Result: J. C. Cobbold, Tory   829
H. E. Adair, Liberal   708
Capt. Gladstone, Tory   661
H. Vincent, Radical   546

The following table is based on the pollbook in Manchester University Library.

Selected categories	Vincent	Adair	Cobbold	Gladstone
Gentlemen	17	33	54	48
Bankers	1	1	3	2
Lawyers	2	6	12	12
Physicians	4	7	15	12
Dissenting ministers	8	8	0	0
R.C. priest	0	1	0	0
Brewers	8	8	3	3
Publicans and beersellers	17	30	55	46
Farmers	6	7	34	32
Grocers	29	31	14	10
Butchers	10	16	20	19
Shoemakers	25	28	18	14
Shipwrights	9	7	8	6
Mariners	23	27	22	20
Master mariners	0	2	2	1
Pilots	0	1	4	3
Railwaymen	1	1	5	3
Parish clerk	0	0	1	0
Organists	0	1	2	1

The following analysis is based on the pollbook in the Institute of Historical Research.

Composition of Vincent's vote

Plumps	52
and Adair	453
and Cobbold	29
and Gladstone	12

I. Respectables

Gentlemen	42
Shipbuilders	4
Merchants, etc.	26
Brewers	8
Surgeons	4
Banker	1
Builders	4
Dissenting ministers	8
Police officer	1
Coachmakers	4
Schoolmasters	3
Shipowner	1
Maltsters	4
Commercial professions	22
Farmers	6
	138

II. Trade

Shopkeepers	119
Milkmen	4
Publicans	10
Beersellers	8
	141

The Ipswich election of 1847 (cont.)

III. Crafts

		Woodworkers	53
Shoemakers	24		221
Tailors	29		
Building, etc.	19	IV. Others	
Metal crafts	29	Cordwainers and servants	13
Shipwrights	9	Labourers	24
Minor crafts	37	Miscellaneous	7
Mariners	21		44

The Ipswich election of 1852

The pollbook is in the Institute of Historical Research.

Result: J. C. Cobbold, Conservative 810
H. E. Adair, Liberal 784
S. Bateson, Conservative 727
T. B. Hobhouse, Liberal 725

Selected categories	Adair	Hobhouse	Cobbold	Bateson
Clergymen	3	1	12	11
Parish clerk	0	0	1	1
Organist	1	0	1	0
Dissenting ministers	6	6	0	0
Gentlemen	46	41	67	64
Lawyers	7	5	17	16
Surgeons	6	5	15	14
Bankers	3	3	2	2
Farmers	11	9	35	31
Publicans	25	24	37	32
Beersellers	6	5	5	3
Brewers	8	7	3	3
Mariners	21	21	32	32
Shipwrights	7	6	8	7
Pilots	0	0	3	3
Butchers	19	18	16	15
Grocers	30	28	21	16
Shoemakers	30	29	16	18
Railwaymen	1	2	9	8
Labourers	22	21	7	5

The Ipswich election of 1857

The pollbook is in the Institute of Historical Research.

Result: J. C. Cobbold, Conservative 779
H. E. Adair, Liberal 759
J. C. Marshman, Liberal 738
H. J. Selwin, Conservative 707

Selected categories	Adair	Marshman	Cobbold	Selwin
Clergymen	2	2	3	3
Organists	1	1	1	1
Sexton	0	0	1	1

I

The Ipswich election of 1857 (cont.)

Selected categories	Adair	Marshman	Cobbold	Selwin
R.C. priest	1	0	0	0
Dissenting ministers	7	7	0	0
Surgeons	7	6	16	16
Bankers	3	3	1	1
Ironfounders	7	7	2	2
Mariners	16	15	22	19
Shipwrights	3	8	9	3
Pilots	0	0	4	4
Railwaymen	4	4	7	5
Labourers	15	15	6	6

The Ipswich election of 1859

The pollbook is in the Institute of Historical Research.

Result: J. C. Cobbold, Conservative 915
H. E. Adair, Liberal 862
H. J. Selwin, Conservative 837
John King, Liberal 386

Selected categories	Adair	King	Cobbold	Selwin
Dissenting ministers	7	4	0	0
R.C. priest	1	0	0	0
Organist	0	0	1	1
Sexton	0	0	1	1
Officers	1	0	5	4
Pilots	0	0	4	4
Mariners	14	7	41	38
Shipwrights	4	1	14	13
Brewers	7	1	3	3
Publicans	39	13	78	76
Gentlemen	92	42	99	90
Lawyers	8	3	24	23
Surgeons	6	2	17	17
Bankers	3	0	4	4
Ironfounders	11	4	5	5
Farmers	13	7	26	24
Grocers	33	17	23	21
Butchers	20	11	15	15
Shoemakers	33	26	21	16
Railway personnel*	4	0	5	4
Tailors	29	18	12	10
Labourers	23	8	11	12
Carpenters	23	13	21	21
Harbourmaster	1	1	0	0

* The stationmaster plumped for Adair.

There were two manufacturers of shoes who voted Liberal; none voted Tory. Probably some of the shoemakers listed above were their employees.

The Ipswich election of 1859 (cont.)

Analysis of the vote

Plumps			Splits	
Adair	354	Adair and King	382
Cobbold	9	Adair and Cobbold	104
Selwin	14	Adair and Selwin	21
King	4	Cobbold and Selwin	802
		King and Cobbold	0
		King and Selwin	0

A prefatory letter by Adair contains this remark: '...and I gratefully acknowledge the active cooperation and assistance which I have received from the Non-Electors of this Borough.'

The Ipswich election of 1865

The pollbook is in the Institute of Historical Research.

Result: H. E. Adair, Liberal   990
J. C. Cobbold, Conservative 913
West, Liberal   905
Tidmas, Conservative   776

Selected categories	West	Tidmas
Gentlemen	86	81
Bankers	2	2
Surgeons or physicians	9	17
Brewers	11	5
Publicans	36	71
Beersellers	2	5
Railwaymen	2	4
Grocers	30	24
Shoemakers	31	16
Dissenting clergy	9	0
Sexton	0	1
R.C. priest*	0	1
Fisherman	1	0
Pilot	0	1
Shipwrights	6	4
Sailmakers	1	2
Engineers	13	4
Machinists	3	0
Mariners	9	24
Boatbuilder	1	0
Shipowners	3	1
Saddlers	6	4
Shipbuilders	1	1
Ironfounders	4	3
Boilermaker	1	0
Foundrymen	2	0
Waterman	0	1

* The priest voted for both Tory candidates.

The Ipswich election of 1868

The pollbook is in the Institute of Historical Research.

Result:	H. E. Adair, Liberal	2,321
	West, Liberal	2,195
	J. C. Cobbold, Conservative	2,044

Selected categories	Adair	Cobbold
Gentlemen	118	100
Bankers	3	1
Surgeons or physicians	11	14
Brewers	6	6
Publicans	15	71
Beersellers	10	19
Railwaymen	32	31
Bargeman	0	1
Labourers	186	160
Shoemakers	134	37
Turnkeys	5	2
Sweeps	0	4
Dissenting ministers	9	0
Anglican clergy	0	14
R.C. priest	0	1
Saddlers	5	4
Mariners	32	140
Shipwrights	6	38
Pilots	0	8
Pilot master	0	1
Ship carpenters	0	2
Sailmakers	3	7
Boilermakers	12	0
Mastmakers	0	2
Foundrymen	10	1
Fishermen	2	4
Ironfounders	8	5
Postmen	5	7
Lightermen	0	2
Exciseman	0	1
Dredgerman	0	1
Watermen	0	5

The Lancaster election of 1865

The pollbook is in Manchester Public Library. No clerical votes were recorded in the pollbook. Occupations were only stated for the freemen voters (about 1,000), not for the £10 householders (about 300).

Result: Fenwick, Liberal   713
         Schneider, Liberal   687
         Lawrence, Conservative 665

Freemen only:

selected categories	Fenwick	Lawrence
Gentlemen	17	25
Surgeons	1	2
Lawyers	4	10
Farmers	24	54
Innkeepers	2	3
Railway employees*	4	2
Shoemakers	20	11
Weavers†	7	1
Woolcombers	4	2
Cotton spinners	7	3
Silk spinners	6	2
Silk piecers	3	1
Silk combers	3	0
Silk boiler	1	0
Silk dressers	4	1

* The stationmaster voted Tory.

† All engaged in textile occupations are listed in the table.

The most numerous classes not listed in the table were fishermen, mariners, husbandmen, labourers, and metal craftsmen.

Plumps		Splits	
Fenwick	2	Fenwick and Schneider	670
Schneider	2	Lawrence and Fenwick	41
Lawrence	609	Schneider and Lawrence	15

Of these, the £10 householders voted thus:

          Fenwick   252
          Schneider   244
          Lawrence   170

The freemen voted thus:

	Town	Country
Fenwick	308	153
Schneider	299	144
Lawrence	295	200

          No. on Register 1,419
          No. voted   1,339
          Turnout   94 %

The Leeds election of 1834

Result: Edward Baines, Liberal	1,951
Sir J. Beckett, Conservative	1,917
Joshua Bower, Liberal	24

The votes analysed are those polled in Leeds township proper, which included about three-quarters of the electorate. Only those voters with names beginning A to M inclusive were analysed: it was felt that this was a sufficient and typical sample. About 400 voters of unclassifiable or unstated occupation, fairly evenly divided between parties, are not listed.

Leeds township

I. Occupations unconnected with textiles	Liberal	Conservative
Brewers and maltsters	6	3
Publicans	25	47
Beersellers	4	7
Shopkeepers	139	120
Building crafts	31	24
Metal crafts	43	24
Minor crafts	50	30
Shoemakers	11	6
Tailors	16	18
Gentlemen	21	36
Military and Naval officers	1	2
Medical	4	19
Legal	8	16
Bankers	1	4
Schoolmasters	9	8
Printers	9	0
Farmers	2	6
Commercial professions	34	40
General merchants	69	69
Builders	3	14
Mustard manufacturer	0	1
Servants, labourers	7	18
Anglican clergy	0	7
Sexton	0	1
Comb manufacturer	1	0
Tobacco manufacturers	4	0
II. Textile vote		
Callenderers*	2	0
Textile merchants	30	12
Woolstaplers	15	15
Dyers*	24	19
Cloth dressers*	10	4
Flax dressers*	2	2
Flax spinners*	4	0
Worsted spinner*	1	0

* Probably operatives.

The Leeds election of 1834 (cont.)

	Liberal	Conservative
II. Textile votes (*cont.*)		
Woolsorters*	3	0
Cloth drawers*	2	0
Overlookers*	5	3
Stuff manufacturers	5	2
Cloth manufacturers	8	8
Cloth glosser*	1	0
Linen manufacturers	1	1
Woollen printer*	1	0
Carpet manufacturers	0	2
Stocking manufacturer	0	1
Buckram manufacturer	0	1
Worsted manufacturers	1	1
Cloth miller	0	1
Stuff dresser	0	1
Stuff printer	0	1
Flax manufacturers	2	1
	117	75

* Probably operatives.

The following table gives an exhaustive analysis of the votes polled for the Out-townships of Leeds (Hunslet, Holbeck, Beeston, Wortley, Armley, Farnley, Bramley, Headingley, Potternewton, and Chapel Allerton).

Out-townships

I. Occupations unconnected with textiles	Liberal	Conservative
Building and wood crafts	20	28
Metal crafts	36	26
Minor crafts	20	17
Shoemakers	16	2
Tailors	8	1
Anglican clergy	0	7
Dissenting minister	1	0
Methodist minister	1	0
Schoolmasters	5	3
Publicans	19	47
Beersellers	10	11
Brewers and maltsters	18	18
Gentlemen	16	32
Medical	5	3
Legal	0	3
Bankers	1	1
Official and commercial	16	14
Farmers	15	91
Servants, labourers	15	23
Miscellaneous	47	38
Shopkeepers	82	48
Merchants, wholesalers	17	25
Tobacco manufacturer	0	1

The Leeds election of 1834 (cont.)

II. Textile votes	Liberal	Conservative
Cloth manufacturer	62	46
Clothiers	99	84
Cloth makers	4	2
Woolsorters*	1	2
Dyers*	4	3
Textile merchants	6	6
Overlookers*	5	1
'Manufacturers'	21	37
Slubbers*	1	1
Cloth dressers*	0	2
Cloth drawers*	4	0
Cloth millers*	2	0
Bleacher	1	0
Silk manufacturer	1	0
Flax manufacturer	1	0
Flax spinners*	5	0
Woolstapler	3	0
	220	184

* Probably operatives.

The Leeds election of 1847

The pollbook is in the Bodleian Library. Occupations are not stated, but the type of property qualifying a voter is included.

Result:	Wm. Beckett, Conservative	2,529
	J. G. Marshall, Whig	2,172
	Joseph Sturge, Radical	1,978

Selected categories of property	Sturge	Marshall	Beckett
Factory or Mill	112	75	85
Foundry, machine shop	11	15	12
Sawmill	2	3	3
Chemical works	4	5	3
Dyehouse	11	20	22
Quarry	1	2	3
Tanhouse	0	1	1
Coalpit	0	1	1

Some types of commercial or productive property—warehouses, brewhouses, offices, maltkilns, and small workshops—are not included in the above table, though data were available. Nevertheless, this table is a sufficient and illuminating indication of the extent to which the Leeds business world supported Sturge's pacifist radicalism.

The Leicester Borough election of 1832

The pollbook is in the Guildhall Library.

Result: Evans, Liberal   1,663 (of whom 256 were non-resident)
       Wynn Ellis, Liberal   1,527 (of whom 226 were non-resident)
       Boughton Leigh, Conservative 1,266 (of whom 243 were non-resident)

Resident voters: selected categories	Evans	Ellis	Leigh
Clergy	0	0	2
Dissenting ministers	5	5	0
Parish clerks	1	0	2
Engineers	1	2	0
Woolstaplers	15	15	5
Manufacturer	0	0	1
Shoemakers	43	45	35
Gentlemen	43	28	71
Framework knitters	273	270	83

The Leicester Borough election of 1847

The pollbook is in the Guildhall Library.

Result: Sir J. Walmesley, Liberal   1,657
       R. Gardner, Liberal   1,614
       Jas. Parker, Conservative   1,423

The non-resident freemen voters (who are omitted from the analysis) polled: for Walmesley 130, for Gardner 127, for Parker 239.

Resident voters: selected categories	Walmesley	Gardner	Parker
Surgeons	8	7	17
Shoemakers	62	62	44
Framework knitters	233	238	81
Labourers	17	17	30
Butchers	23	23	36
Grocers	66	63	31
Clergymen	0	0	5
Dissenting ministers	6	6	1
Clerk to Leicester Union	0	0	1
Woolstaplers	2	2	0
Engineers	7	7	0
Policemen	8	8	0
Gentlemen	61	64	112
Ironfounders	3	3	2
Sexton	1	0	1
Manufacturers	14	14	3
Banker	0	0	1
Gaoler	0	0	1
R.C. priest	1	1	0

The Leicester election of 1859

The pollbook is in the Guildhall Library.

Result: John Biggs, Liberal   1,584
     J. W. Noble, Liberal   1,496
     W. U. Heygate, Conservative   1,479
     J. D. Harris, Liberal   1,397

Whole pollbook

Selected categories	Biggs	Noble	Harris	Heygate
Anglican clergy	2	2	6	9
Ministers	4	0	8	0
Parish clerk	0	0	0	1
Methodist minister	0	0	1	0
Organist	0	1	0	1
Baptist minister	0	0	1	1
Saddlers	1	2	2	4
Ironfounders	2	3	6	7
Engineers	9	6	7	4
Bankers	1	0	2	2
Surgeons	7	14	12	15
Warp hands	11	11	6	2
Labourers	8	17	28	41
Shoe manufacturers	6	6	2	2
Framesmiths	30	24	14	5
Loomhands	4	2	8	1
Woolstaplers	20	13	15	10
Framework knitters	205	201	56	63
Manufacturers	59	43	38	26
Woolcombers	21	17	8	5
Spinners	12	5	17	9
Beersellers	9	15	2	5

Electors of first four wards only
(pages 1–33 only of pollbook)

Selected categories	Biggs	Noble	Harris	Heygate
Gentlemen	32	19	47	51
Shoemakers	33	31	12	13
Hosiers	17	15	24	21
Grocers	42	33	40	30
Butchers	21	30	10	31
Victuallers	53	72	3	51
Warehousemen	5	5	8	5

The Leicester Borough by-election of 1861

Result: W. U. Heygate, Conservative   1,596
     J. D. Harris, Liberal   1,033
     P. A. Taylor, Liberal   977

Those in the first table below were analysed only for pages 1–13, or the first four wards, of the pollbook, and may therefore be untypical, though there is no

The Leicester Borough by-election of 1861 (cont.)

special reason to think so. Those in the second table were analysed for the whole of the pollbook, including out-voters. The occupations of about 50 people were omitted by the pollbook.

Selected categories	Harris	Taylor	Heygate
Gentlemen	4	5	13
Shoemakers	11	18	6
Victuallers	2	29	28
Framework knitters	23	60	18
Shoe manufacturers	1	4	4

Selected categories	Harris	Taylor	Heygate
Surgeons	8	3	13
Manufacturers	55	23	22
Labourers	4	11	62*
Dissenting ministers	14	1	2
Engineers	6	3	4
Railwaymen	0	0	1
Clergymen	1	0	6
Parish clerk	0	0	1
Turnkeys	0	0	2
Ironfounders	3	0	3

* These labourers were mostly non-resident freemen voters from the villages

The Leicestershire election of August 1830

The pollbook is in the Institute of Historical Research.

Result: G. A. L. Keck, Conservative   3,517⎱
      Lord Robert Manners, Conservative   3,000⎰ sitting members
      Thomas Paget, Liberal   2,203

The last contested election had been in 1775.

Selected categories	Paget	Keck	Manners
Physicians	14	37	32
Officers	0	3	3
Bankers	1	5	5
Dissenting ministers	13	4	2
Parish clerks	0	4	4
Anglican clergy	8	147	143
Worsted spinners	15	10	4
Woolcombers	9	7	3
Woolstaplers	9	15	11
Weavers	8	12	12
Lace manufacturers	33	7	5
Lace makers	39	11	6
Hosiers	67	45	31
Framework knitters	245	143	87

The Leicestershire (South) election of 1841

The pollbook is in the Guildhall Library. It does not give occupations of voters, but the names of clergy are indicated by the prefix 'Rev.'.

Result: H. Halford, Conservative   2,638
C. W. Packe, Conservative   2,622
T. Gisborne, Liberal   1,213
Col. E. H. Cheney, Liberal   1,196

	Gisborne	Cheney	Halford	Packe	Abstained
Clergy	2	2	40	40	28

The Leicestershire (South) election of 1867

The pollbook is in the Guildhall Library. It does not give occupations of voters.

Result: T. T. Paget, Liberal   2,302
A. Pell, Conservative   2,263

	Paget	Pell	Abstained
Clergy	20	78	16

The Lewes election of 1835 |

The pollbook is in the Library of the Society of Genealogists.

Result: Sir Charles R. Blunt, Liberal   511
Thomas R. Kemp, Liberal   382
Hon. Henry Fitzroy, Conservative 359

Selected categories	Blunt	Kemp	Fitzroy
Gentlemen	24	23	12
Clergymen	1	1	3
Dissenting ministers	4	4	0
Surgeons	5	3	4
Lawyers	3	3	4
Bankers	1	1	2
Grocers	13	8	7
Publicans	11	10	7
Beersellers	2	1	5
Shoemakers	26	24	11
Painters	2	1	4
Turnkeys	0	1	2
Labourers	24	4	26

The Lewes by-election of 1837

The pollbook is in the Library of the Society of Genealogists.

Result: Hon. H. Fitzroy, Conservative   397
        John Easthope, Liberal   371

Selected categories	Easthope	Fitzroy
Gentlemen	24	22
Clergymen	0	4
Dissenting ministers	4	1
Surgeons	1	5
Lawyers	6	4
Bankers	1	2
Millers	3	2
Grocers	7	11
Butchers	11	12
Publicans	9	7
Beersellers	2	3
Shoemakers	27	18
Tailors	17	12
Carpenters	29	11
Painters	4	6
Parish clerk	0	1
Bargemasters	1	1
Bargemen	6	2
Turnkeys	0	3
Labourers	14	17

The Lewes election of 1841

The pollbook is in the Guildhall Library.

Result: Summers Harford, Liberal   411
       H. Elphinstone, Liberal   409
       Hon. Henry Fitzroy, Conservative 407
       Viscount Cantilupe, Conservative 388

On petition Mr Harford was unseated.

Selected categories	Harford	Elphinstone	Fitzroy	Cantilupe
Gentlemen	21	21	24	24
Lawyers	5	5	5	5
Surgeons	2	2	5	5
Bankers	1	1	2	2
Parish clerks	0	1	2	1
Farmers	2	2	5	4
Dissenting ministers	2	2	1	1
Innkeepers	10	9	9	8
Beersellers	4	4	2	2
Shoemakers	29	26	24	18
Carpenters	31	33	11	11
Butchers	12	13	10	9

The Lewes election of 1841 (cont.)

Selected categories	Harford	Elphinstone	Fitzroy	Cantilupe
Grocers	8	8	11	11
Turnkeys	1	0	5	4
Bargemasters	1	0	2	2
Bargemen	5	5	1	1

The Lincoln City election of 1835

The pollbook is in the Guildhall Library.

Result: Sibthorp, Conservative 565
Bulwer, Liberal 466
Phipps, Liberal 335

Freemen only:* selected categories	Bulwer	Phipps	Sibthorp
Surgeons	1	1	4
Shoemakers	13	9	20
Butchers	6	5	9
Grocers	8	7	6
Clergymen	2	1	5
Farmers	4	3	33
Labourers	9	6	38
Watermen	6	4	11
Sheriff's officers	1	1	2
Aldermen	3	3	7
Mayor	0	0	1

* The table excludes £10 householders, whose occupations were not stated.

The Lincoln City election of 1841

The pollbook is in the Guildhall Library.

Result: Sibthorp, Conservative 541
Collett, Conservative 481
Bulwer, Liberal 443
Seely, Liberal 340

Freemen only: selected categories	Bulwer	Sibthorp	Collett	Seely
Surgeons	1	3	2	0
Shoemakers	17	22	24	11
Butchers	4	6	5	3
Grocers	7	6	4	6
Clergy	0	1	1	0
Farmers	11	23	17	5
Labourers	11	40	42	10
Watermen	5	7	7	5
Sheriff's officer	0	1	1	0

The Lincoln City election of 1848

The pollbook is in the Guildhall Library.

Result: Thomas B. Hobhouse, Liberal   552
L. C. Humphrey, Conservative   550

Freemen only:

selected categories	Hobhouse	Humphrey
Surgeons	0	3
Shoemakers	16	18
Butchers	6	7
Grocers	1	5
Farmers	5	16
Watermen	11	5
Town clerk	1	0
Labourers	25	33

The Lincoln City election of 1859

The pollbook is in the Bodleian Library.

Result: Sibthorp, Conservative   740
Heneage, Liberal   658
Palmer, Liberal   629

Freemen only:

selected categories	Heneage	Palmer	Sibthorp
Shoemakers	17	11	20
Gentlemen	7	2	7
Grocers	3	0	4
Farmers	17	2	15
Labourers	23	22	31
Publicans	4	1	3
Lawyers	5	0	7
Stonemasons	4	3	5
Basketmakers	0	3	0
Ironmoulder	0	1	0
Tailors	6	6	6
Watermen	5	5	4
Butchers	9	3	9
Merchants	6	3	6
Surgeons	3	0	4

The Lincoln City election of 1862

The pollbook is in the Bodleian Library.

Result: J. B. Moore, Conservative   715
        J. H. Palmer, Liberal   690

Freemen only: selected categories	Palmer	Moore
Shoemakers	14	16
Grocers	0	7
Farmers	5	18
Labourers	27	43
Publicans	1	3
Boilermakers	5	0
Stonemasons	3	5
Basketmakers	5	0
Ironmoulder	1	0
Tailors	9	7
Gentlemen	3	8
Watermen	2	8
Butchers	7	8
Lawyers	0	7
Merchants	2	5
Surgeons	0	6
Turnkey	0	1

The Lincoln City election of 1865

The pollbook is in the Bodleian Library.

Result: C. Seely, Liberal   878
        E. Heneage, Liberal   870
        J. B. Moore, Conservative 765

Freemen only: selected categories	Seely	Heneage	Moore
Shoemakers	14	14	18
Grocers	1	2	5
Farmers	9	12	12
Lawyers	0	0	6
Labourers	50	52	34
Publicans	3	3	4
Basketmakers	4	4	1
Ironmoulders	2	2	0
Tailors	8	9	8
Gentlemen	4	6	7
Watermen	6	6	6
Butchers	7	8	8
Boilermakers	3	3	0
Stonemasons	4	3	3
Merchants	7	7	4
Surgeons	1	3	6
Turnkey	0	0	1

The Lincolnshire by-election of 1823

The pollbook is in Peterborough Public Library.

Result: Ingilby   3,816
        Thorold   1,575

Ingilby represented the Whig influence of the Yarborough family, and Thorold campaigned in the name of the independence of the freeholders. The following analysis by hundreds is instructive in showing the territorial character of electoral allegiance.

	Ingilby	Thorold
Holland		
Skirbeck	205	99
Kirton	165	54
Elloe	181	37
Kesteven		
Boothby Graffoe	21	142
Langoe*	99	94
Flaxwell	34	73
Aswardhurn	14	83
Winnibriggs	3	68
Soke of Grantham	1	132
Loveden	5	226
Lindsey		
Manley	611	22
Yarborough	431	6
Bradley	175	5
Ludborough	13	2
Louth Eske	220	31
Walshcroft	145	4
Calceworth	144	13
Candleshoe	164	4
Wraggoe	44	19
Gartree	85	38
Horncastle	151	37
Hill	60	1
Bolingbroke	139	13
Aslacoe	?	?
Well	48	27
Lawres	192	23
Corringham	268	62
Aveland	19	105
Beltisloe	7	47
Ness	22	49

Even when one takes a hundred which was apparently evenly divided, a further breakdown reveals that this even division arises mainly from a chance equality between groups of villages which themselves voted largely en bloc.

* See following table.

K

The Lincolnshire by-election of 1823 (cont.)

Analysis of Langoe Hundred in Kesteven by villages

	Ingilby	Thorold
Billinghay	1	49
Blankney	3	0
Dunston	6	0
Dogdike	3	3
Heighington	23	0
Kyme	1	7
Hanworth	6	1
Kirkby Green	1	0
Metheringham	9	7
Martin	11	1
Necton	1	0
Scopwick	6	0
Timberland	4	7
Walcot	8	20
Washingborough	17	0

The Lincolnshire (South) election of 1841

The pollbook is in the Guildhall Library. It does not state the occupations of voters.

Result:		
C. Turnor, Conservative		4,579
Sir John Trollope, Bt., Conservative		4,564
Henry Handley, Liberal		2,960

	Handley	Turnor	Trollope
Clergy	16	106	109

The Lindsey election of 1835

The pollbook is in the Guildhall Library.

Result:		
Hon. C. A. W. Pelham, Liberal		4,489
T. G. Corbett, Conservative		4,450
Sir W. A. Ingilby, Bt., Liberal		3,984

Selected categories	Pelham	Ingilby	Corbett
Parish clerks	26	14	39
Cordwainers	73	87	57
Clergymen	75	15	148
Ministers	5	9	1
Surgeons	30	22	30
Grocers	46	46	35
Merchants	22	21	32
Weavers	15	17	19
Engineers	2	2	1
Fishermen	6	0	4
R.C. priests	2	1	0
Shipbuilder	0	1	0
Machine maker	1	1	0
Gaolers	2	0	2

The Lindsey election of 1835 (cont.)

The introduction to the pollbook states: '...in every town throughout the county, committees of tradesmen were formed to secure the return of Sir William Ingilby: to counteract this, the principal farmers in most parishes exerted themselves with an ardour worthy of the cause they espoused, and to the exertions of the agriculturists, and the agriculturists alone, is this glorious victory to be attributed.'

The Lindsey election of 1852

Result: The Rt. Hon. R. A. Christopher, Conservative — 5,585
J. B. Stanhope, Conservative — 5,577
Sir M. Cholmeley, Liberal — 4,777

For about one-third of the total number of electors in the pollbook, no particulars of occupations are stated. The voting recorded below therefore might not be typical of the whole constituency: though there is no special reason to suggest this. The figures for clergymen are however probably nearly comprehensive, being based on the prefix 'Rev.' appearing before the name.

Selected categories	Stanhope	Cholmeley	Christopher
Pages 1–22 of pollbook			
Farmers	217	165	250
Millers	3	7	7
Brewers	4	2	4
Innkeepers	8	11	12
Clergymen	11	1	13
Parish clerks	2	1	3
Dissenting ministers	0	2	0
Surgeons	4	2	4
Lawyers	5	6	6
Grocers	2	6	3
Butchers	11	8	13
Tailors	5	13	6
Cordwainers	3	9	8
Mariners	1	6	0
Whole pollbook			
Clergymen	133	60	170
Parish clerks	9	7	10
Dissenting ministers	0	3	0
Surgeons	15	17	19
Lawyers	27	19	29
Millers	29	40	35
Brewers	8	10	7
Innkeepers	64	59	65
Grocers	30	30	32
Butchers	30	32	37
Tailors	20	44	22
Cordwainers	41	70	41
Mariners	1	17	2

Plumps		Splits	
Christopher	158	Christopher and Stanhope	4,578
Stanhope	115	Christopher and Cholmeley	850
Cholmeley	3,037	Stanhope and Cholmeley	882

The Liverpool by-election of November 1830*

The pollbook is in the Institute of Historical Research. It gives (page 80) its own occupational analysis of voting which, slightly abridged, is as follows:

Result:† J. E. Denison, Tory   2,106
Wm. Ewart, Reformer 2,019

Out-voters: Ewart   345
Denison   367

	Ewart	Denison
Gentlemen, merchants, brokers	241	382
Accountants, bookkeepers	79	67
Printers, stationers, etc.	24	24
Shipwrights, boatbuilders	297	249
Sailmakers	89	98
Coopers	164	170
Mariners, pilots, riggers‡	67	104
Ropers, flaxdressers, etc.	129	148
Blockmakers	55	86
Woodworkers	228	139
Painters, plumbers	66	58
Ironmongers, smiths	59	62
Masons, bricklayers	128	115
Cordwainers	57	26
Jewellers, watchmakers	64	40
Butchers, bakers	33	44
Tallow chandlers	23	24
Brushmakers, tobacconists	34	34
Barbers, tailors, drapers	32	29
Hatters, saddlers, pawnbrokers	38	28
Ironfounders, engineers	47	24
Curriers and tanners	229§	7
Braziers and tinmen	37	28
Potters, pipemakers	16	12
Labourers, servants	36	23
Druggists, silversmiths	15	13
Dyers, furriers	17	13
Teachers	14	15
Hosiers	14	17
Divers others	94	113
	2,019	2,106

* On the death of Mr Huskisson.
† Other authorities such as Bean and Dod give the result as Ewart, Whig, 2,215, Denison, Whig, 2,186.
‡ According to my own calculations from the pollbook, the pilots voted as follows:

Ewart   9
Denison   39

§ This figure is certainly wildly wrong.

The Liverpool election of 1832

Result: Ewart, Liberal   4,931
Lord Sandon, Conservative   4,260
Thornely, Liberal   4,096
Sir H. Douglas, Conservative   3,249

The voting of the following occupations was only analysed as far as the bottom of page 44 of the pollbook (to the name 'Isaac, John Edmund'), and there abandoned as a sufficiently large and typical sample of the whole.

	Ewart	Thornely	Sandon	Douglas
Gentlemen	128	107	84	61
Merchants	151	118	175	135
Grocers	53	42	19	10

All the votes cast by the members of the occupations below have been analysed as follows:

I. Manufacture	Ewart	Thornely	Sandon	Douglas
Sugar refiners	4	4	4	4
Soap manufacturers	6	6	4	4
Glass manufacturers	1	1	4	4
Tobacco manufacturers	7	5	4	3
Ironfounders	21	18	15	13
Organbuilders	2	1	1	3
II. Mercantile				
Bankers	13	11	13	8
Corn merchants	20	20	9	6
Cotton brokers	18	17	13	11
Timber merchants	27	24	26	24
III. Professions				
Clergy and ministers*	20	16	33	28
Surgeons, physicians	66	57	41	30
Lawyers	24	18	36	29
Royal Navy	3	3	9	6
Architects	7	7	9	8
Organists	0	0	2	2
Sexton	0	0	1	1
IV.				
Innkeepers	316	269	118	63
Tailors	94	81	52	29
Butchers	58	48	47	29
Farmers	3	3	2	2
V. Marine				
Master mariners	14	9	24	16
Mariners	57	51	71	59
Sailmakers	61	47	86	76
Pilots	11	6	34	23
Shipwrights†	61	39	320	287

* The Rev. Jabez Bunting, the 'Methodist Pope', plumped for Lord Sandon. The future radicals, William Rathbone and Robertson Gladstone, on this occasion each split their votes between Sandon and Ewart.

† This includes only shipwrights voting by virtue of a qualification as freemen. The very few shipwrights voting as £10 householders have been omitted.

The Liverpool election of 1832 (cont.)

Summary

The pollbook itself contains a general summary of voting at this election, which is reproduced here as it stands. No detailed breakdown was given in the pollbook.

A. Gentry, clergy, merchants, bankers, brokers, medical and legal professions, wine merchants and wholesale dealers:

Ewart, Liberal	1,134
Thornely, Liberal	922
Sandon, Conservative	1,187
Douglas, Conservative	912

B. Tradesmen including innkeepers

Ewart	2,244
Thornely	1,859
Sandon	1,322
Douglas	945

C. Mechanics, shipwrights, coopers, sailmakers, etc.

Ewart	1,553
Thornely	1,315
Sandon	1,751
Douglas	1,392

The Liverpool election of 1835

The pollbook is in the Institute of Historical Research.

Result:		
Lord Sandon, Conservative	4,407
Wm. Ewart, Liberal	4,075
Sir Howard Douglas, Bt., Conservative	3,869
James Morris, Liberal	3,627

Selected categories	Ewart	Morris	Sandon	Douglas
Anglican clergy	4	5	30	27
Dissenting ministers	13	13	2	1
Servants	0	0	4	3
Labourers*	89	76	60	54
Curriers	7	6	6	5
Bankers	7	5	9	7
Surgeons	48	45	42	37
Jewish Rabbi	1	1	0	0
Pilots	6	1	33	28
R.C. priests	4	4	0	0
Police	0	0	3	3
Sexton	0	0	1	1

* Freemen labourers were markedly Tory, non-freemen labourers (£10 householders) markedly Liberal.

The Liverpool election of 1835 (cont.)

Selected categories	Ewart	Morris	Sandon	Douglas
Borough officers	0	0	2	2
Turnkey	1	0	1	0
Freemen sailmakers	37	28	93	89
Non-freemen sailmakers (£10 householders)	11	9	6	4
Shipowners	6	7	6	5
Shipbuilders	4	4	14	12
Shipbrokers	4	4	3	3
Boatbuilders*	3	2	18	17
Merchants (freemen)	46	45	123	118
Merchants (non-freemen)	242	236	336	293
Shipwrights (freemen)	29	20	326	325
Shipwrights (non-freemen)	7	8	23	20

* All boatbuilders were freemen voters, not £10 householders.

The Liverpool election of 1841

The pollbook is in the Institute of Historical Research.

Result: Viscount Sandon, Conservative   5,979
Cresswell Creswell, Conservative   5,792
Sir Joshua Walmsley, Liberal   4,647
Lord Palmerston, Liberal   4,431

Selected categories	Walmsley	Palmerston	Sandon	Creswell
Anglican clergy	5	5	42	42
Surgeons	61	59	73	67
Dissenting ministers	13	13	0	0
Bankers	7	8	11	11
Officers	2	2	6	6
Policemen	2	1	6	6
Stevedores	6	6	3	3
Turnkeys	0	0	2	2
Sextons	0	0	2	2
Parish clerks	0	0	2	2
Pilots	1	2	65	65
Sailmakers	27	25	85	82
Shipowners	6	6	13	13
Shipbrokers	8	7	13	11
Shipbuilders	4	4	18	18
Shipwrights	67	62	350	346

An example of the non-industrial character of London extreme radicalism

The following analysis of the membership of the West End section of the International Workingmen's Association, the 'First International', is based on a manuscript of 29 March 1873 in the Jung Nachlass, item no. 165, in the Instituut voor Soziale Geschedenis, Amsterdam, by whose courtesy it is used.

Bootmakers	6	Furniture decorator	1
Painters	5	Plumber	1
Portmanteau makers	3	Cooperative shopkeeper	1
Carriage wheelwright	1	Blacksmiths	2
Tailors	5	Trunk maker	1
Railway official	1	Unstated	2
Labourer	1		

The Londonderry City election of 1868

Result: Richard Dowse, Q.C., Liberal   705
Lord Claude John Hamilton, Conservative   599

The Times of 27 November 1868 published the following analysis of voting:

	Dowse	Hamilton	Total registered
Catholics	520	15	567
Presbyterians and Dissenters	177	284	601
Church of Ireland	8	300	315

Voting at Loughborough in the Leicestershire election of 1830*

Result: G. A. L. Keck, Tory   3,517⎫
      Lord R. Manners, Tory   3,000⎬ sitting members
      Thos. Paget, Whig   2,203

The last contested election was in 1775.
Taking the voters for Loughborough only:

Keck	102
Manners	72
Paget	139

All voters:	Paget	Keck		Paget	Keck
I. Respectables			Maltsters	0	2
Banker	0	1	Innkeepers	0	3
Nonconformist	1	0	Carriage makers	2	0
clergy			Millers	3	0
Teachers	0	2		10	7
Clerks	0	4	III. Textiles		
Surgeon	0	1			
Auctioneer	1	0	Hosiers	3	1
Gentlemen	6	8	Framework knitters	2	0
Attorney	0	1	Lacemakers	24	1
Servants	4	2	Woolstaplers	1	2
	12	19	Dyers	2	0
II. Business				32	4
Timber merchant	0	1	IV.		
Brick maker	1	1	Yeomen	4	5
Builders	4	0	Farmers	6	18

* See p. 127 above also for the table on the Leics. election of 1830 generally.

Voting at Loughborough in the Leicestershire election of 1830 (cont.)

	Paget	Keck			Paget	Keck
V. Shopkeepers				Blacksmiths	3	o
Grocers	6	2		Roper	o	1
Bakers	3	1		Machinemakers	6	o
Wine merchant	1	1		Building and wood	8	6
Drapers	4	1		Cooper	o	1
Butcher	1	1		Nailmakers	3	o
Chandler	1	o		Brazier	1	o
Druggist	o	1			22	9
	16	7	**VII.**			
VI. Crafts				Labourers	6	4
Tailor	1	1		Miscellaneous	3	4

The Macclesfield election of 1835

The pollbook is in the British Museum. Occupations of voters are not stated directly, but the type of property owned by each elector is given.

Result: John Ryle, Conservative   464
John Brocklehurst, Liberal   424
Thos. Grimsditch, Conservative 342

Type of property	Brocklehurst	Ryle	Grimsditch
Factory	39	42	22
Workshop	7	7	2
Dyehouse	5	6	5
Foundry	2	2	o
Public house	41	56	57

The Maidstone election of 1830

The pollbook is in the Library of the Society of Genealogists.

Result: A. W. Robarts, Whig   470 (227 plumps)
H. Winchester, Tory   387 (237 plumps)
P. Rawlings, Tory   156 (20 plumps)*
W. G. T. D. Tyssen, Whig 6

Alderman Winchester represented the high church, and Robarts the independent interest.

Selected categories	Robarts	Winchester	Rawlings
Gentlemen	27	21	2
Papermakers	44	33	7
Cordwainers	17	12	10
Watermen	53	15	34

Cross votes
Robarts and Winchester 126
Robarts and Rawlings 112

* According to Henry Stooks Smith, Rawlings had 195 votes.

The Maidstone election of 1832

The pollbook is in the Institute of Historical Research.

Result: A. W. Robarts, Liberal   500
Barnett, Liberal   469
Lewis, Conservative   422

There was very little cross voting (or plumping on the Liberal side).

Selected categories	Robarts	Lewis
Gentlemen	35	29
Physicians and surgeons	2	6
Military and Naval	0	1
Banker	0	1
Papermakers	30	22
Grocers	28	6
Tailors	7	6
Victuallers	21	16
Beersellers	2	3
Brewers	4	2
Dissenting ministers	2	0
Wesleyan minister	1	0

The Maidstone election of 1841

The pollbook is in the Institute of Historical Research.

Result: A. J. B. Beresford Hope, Conservative   765
George Dodd, Conservative   725
David Salomons, Liberal   418

Selected categories	Salomons	Hope	Dodd
Clergymen	0	1	1
Sexton	0	1	1
Dissenting ministers	3	0	0
Turnkey	0	1	0
Policemen	2	4	4
Bankers	0	2	2
Surgeons	3	7	7
Victuallers	10	22	19
Beersellers	2	4	4
Farmers	5	22	22
Watermen	19	24	23
Mariners	3	3	4
Labourers	15	55	50
Shoemakers	24	34	31
Butchers	14	18	17
Grocers	16	10	10
Paper manufacturers	0	2	2
Papermakers	31	58	51

The Maidstone by-election of 1853*

The pollbook is in the Institute of Historical Research.

Result:	Wm. Lee, Liberal	748
	Chas. Wykeham Martin, Liberal	738

Selected categories	Lee	Martin
Clergymen	1	9
Surgeons	6	13
Bankers	0	3
Dissenting ministers	6	0
Policemen	1	7
Turnkeys	0	2
Parish clerk	0	1
Officers	0	3
Watermen	17	30
Mariners	4	2
Labourers	41	47
Victuallers	17	20
Beersellers	17	10
Farmers	8	25
Grocers	34	14
Butchers	12	20
Shoemakers	37	26
Paper manufacturers	2	6
Papermakers	47	24

* No analysis of Maidstone voting is possible between 1841 and 1853, as the pollbook for 1852 does not give occupations, and there was no contest in 1847.

Result: 1847	Hope, Conservative ⎫	unopposed
	Dodd, Conservative ⎭	
1852	Whatman, Liberal	844
	Dodd, Conservative	708
	Lee, Liberal	580

The Maidstone election of 1857

The pollbook is in the Institute of Historical Research.

Result:	A. J. Beresford Hope, Conservative	801
	Capt. Edward Scott, Conservative	759
	Wm. Lee, Liberal	689
	H. Mildmay, Liberal	655

Selected categories	Lee	Mildmay	Hope	Scott
Bankers	0	0	3	3
Lawyers	2	2	5	6
Surgeons	8	8	6	7
Officers	1	1	3	3

The Maidstone election of 1857 (cont.)

Selected categories	Lee	Mildmay	Hope	Scott
Clergymen	0	0	2	2
Paper manufacturers	2	2	4	4
Papermakers	42	39	27	22
Victuallers	16	14	26	24
Beersellers	6	5	14	12
Farmers	9	9	25	24
Shoemakers	37	34	30	29
Grocers	37	39	10	13
Butchers	13	11	22	20
Railwaymen	2	2	4	4
Labourers	33	33	58	57
Turnkeys	0	0	2	2
Mariners	3	2	11	10
Watermen	13	11	18	17
Dissenting ministers	2	2	0	0

The Maidstone election of 1859

The pollbook is in the Library of the Society of Genealogists.

Result: Wm. Lee, Liberal   776
Chas. Buxton, Liberal   776
John Wardlaw, Conservative   751
E. V. Harcourt, Conservative   749

Selected categories	Lee	Buxton	Wardlaw	Harcourt
Gentlemen	32	31	49	46
Surgeons and physicians	6	6	8	8
Lawyers	6	6	8	8
Bankers	0	0	5	5
Anglican clergy	0	0	2	2
Dissenting ministers	3	3	0	0
Paper manufacturers	4	4	2	2
Brewers	3	3	6	6
Publicans	17	16	26	25
Beersellers	7	7	17	17
Papermakers	51	51	22	22
Shoemakers	42	41	21	21
Turnkeys	1	0	7	10
Mariners	22	22	19	19

The Maidstone election of 1865

The pollbook is in the Institute of Historical Research.

Result: Lee, Liberal   869
Whatman, Liberal   867
Betts, Conservative   838
Wardlaw, Conservative   801

All but 60 out of 1,696 votes were straight party votes split between the two party candidates.

The table gives a comprehensive analysis of all votes cast for Lee and Betts:

	Liberal	Con-servative
Gentlemen	38	45
Officers, doctors, lawyers	15	29
Dissenting ministers	7	0
Bankers	0	4
Commercial professions*	38	48
Builders, employers	14	11
Merchants, wholesalers†	28	26
Papermakers	62	32
Brewers	4	7
Publicans	22	33
Beersellers	14	21
Shopkeepers	164	144
Tailors	37	20
Shoemakers	41	30
Building and wood trades	126	79
Metal trades	47	65
Minor crafts	72	50
Labourers	65	82
Servants	12	17
Bargeowner	1	0
Mariners	17	22
Prison employees	0	5
Sexton	0	1
Organist	0	1
Scripture-reader	0	1
Miscellaneous	42	58

* Surveyors, clerks, agents, auctioneers, commercial travellers, house agents, accountants, brokers.
† Merchants: coal and corn dealers, millers, marine stores, timber, and general dealers.

The Maidstone election of 1870

The pollbook is in the Institute of Historical Research.

Result: Sir John Lubbock, Liberal   1,504
           Wm. F. White, Conservative   1,402

Selected categories	Liberal	Con-servative
Gentlemen	41	50
Surgeons or physicians	3	13
Bankers	0	3
Schoolmasters	4	5
Brewers	3	5
Publicans	19	25
Beersellers	5	19
Railwaymen*	40	9
Mariners	7	8
Bargemen	3	10
Sweeps	0	3
Prison employees†	0	22
R.C. priest	1	0
Dissenting ministers	7	0
Anglican clergy	0	10
Sexton	0	1
Vestry clerk	0	1

* The Maidstone stationmaster voted Liberal.
† The Deputy Governor of Maidstone Jail voted Tory.

The Manchester election of 1839

The pollbook for the Manchester by-election of 6 September 1839 is in Manchester Public Library. It is more or less alphabetical but it does not give occupations. There is, however, a Manchester Directory for 1840 which gives, *inter alia*, a list of Manchester clergymen, priests and ministers. The names given in the directory were checked against the pollbook with the following results:

Anglican clergy: Tory   11
                 Liberal   1
                 Abstained   36

Other clergy

Baptists: Liberal   2
          Tory   0
          Abstained   1

Independents: Liberal   3
              Tory   0
              Abstained 5

Unitarians: Liberal   3
            Tory   0
            Abstained   3

None of the dozen or so Methodist ministers, and none of the 11 Catholic priests, appear to have voted. The large number of non-voters was largely due

The Manchester election of 1839 (cont.)

to many clergy living outside the narrow boundaries of electoral Manchester, and especially in Salford.

The only Liberal Anglican was a curate. The Collegiate Church provided six Tory votes.

The Newark election of 1830

The pollbook is in the Guildhall Library.

Result: Willoughby   775
Sadler   746
Wilde   652

Willoughby and Sadler represented the interest of the Duke of Newcastle, while Mr Serjeant Wilde stood for the independence of the people.

Voters A–H inclusive only:

selected categories	Willoughby	Sadler	Wilde
Labourers	64	64	66
Shoemakers	12	12	18
Watermen	13	9	17
Surgeons	2	4	2
Clergy	1	1	0
Dissenting minister	0	0	1
Gentlemen	7	6	4
Weavers	1	1	10
Parish clerk	1	1	0
Police	1	1	0

The Newport, Isle of Wight, election of 1852

The pollbook is in the British Museum.

Result: W. Biggs, Liberal   310
W. Massey, Liberal   306
W. H. C. Plowden, Conservative   266
C. W. Martin, Conservative   256

Selected categories	Biggs	Massey	Plowden	Martin
Lacemakers	35	35	1	1
Ministers	2	2	0	0
Tailors	24	24	11	11
Grocers	18	18	12	12
Butchers	14	15	5	5
Gentlemen	8	8	10	11
Millers	2	2	4	4
Carpenters	7	7	7	7
Saddlers	1	1	4	4
Labourers	5	5	10	10
Mariners	8	8	7	7
Sailmakers	1	1	2	2
Servants	0	0	4	4
Town clerk	0	0	1	1
Relieving officer	0	0	1	1
Police inspector	0	0	1	1
Town sergeant	0	0	1	1
Lawyers	3	3	6	5

The Norfolk East election of 1841

The pollbook is in the Bodleian Library.

Result: Edmond Wodehouse, Conservative   3,498
       H. N. Burroughes, Conservative   3,437
       Sir W. Folkes, Bt., Liberal   1,379

This pollbook does not list occupations as such, but Anglican clergy are indicated by the abbreviation 'clk', and these voted as follows:

Burroughes   184
Wodehouse   183
Folkes   13
Abstained*   191

* Many of these lived at a distance from Norfolk.

The Northampton Borough election of 1831

The pollbook (74 pages) is in the Institute of Historical Research.

Result: Sir George Robinson, Liberal   1,570
      Robert Vernon Smith, Liberal   1,279
      Sir R. H. Gunning, Bt., Conservative   1,157
      Jas. Lyon, Conservative   185

Selected categories	Gunning	Lyon	Robinson	Smith
Pages 1–28 of pollbook				
Shoemakers	52	3	221	261
Whole pollbook				
Gentlemen	78	16	54	36
Lawyers	8	3	1	1
Surgeons	10	2	4	2
Bankers	0	0	2	0
Sextons	4	1	1	0
Parish clerks	2	0	0	0
R.C. priest	0	0	1	1
Dissenting ministers	0	0	6	6
Gaolers	4	1	3	0
Watermen	13	0	4	2
Butchers	33	8	31	19
Grocers	10	3	15	13
Publicans	28	4	21	12

The Northampton Borough election of 1852

The pollbook is in the Northamptonshire County Record Office.

Result: R. Vernon Smith, Liberal   858
          R. Currie, Liberal   824
          G. Ward Hunt, Conservative   746
          J. I. Lockhart, Chartist   109

Lockhart's votes were not analysed.

Selected categories	Smith	Currie	Hunt
Engineers	6	6	0
Shoemakers	191	202	75
Shoe manufacturers	63	64	12
Iron founders	1	1	3
Foundrymen	9	8	9
Railway employees	0	0	5
Labourers	14	9	44
Merchants	4	4	0
Druggists	4	3	10
Publicans	41	39	37
Grocers	11	12	11
Butchers	21	18	29
Gentlemen	25	23	13
Servants	1	1	3
Solicitors	5	4	15
Surgeons	6	6	10
Bankers	1	1	0
Farmers	1	1	5
Dissenting ministers	5	5	1
Anglican clergy	1	0	6
Sweeps	1	2	2
Police	2	1	1
Clerk	0	0	1
Organbuilder	0	0	1
Rate collectors	0	0	2
Registrar	0	0	1
Postboys	0	0	2
Saddlers	2	1	6
Sextons	0	0	2
Relieving officer	0	0	1
Turnkey	0	0	1
Parish clerk	0	0	1

Those abstaining included 2 Dissenting ministers, 4 Anglican clergy, and the Catholic bishop.

L

The Northamptonshire election of 1831

The pollbook is in the Guildhall Library. The following analysis was printed by the compilers of the pollbook and is reproduced here unabridged.

Result: Althorp (A), Reformer   2,462
Milton (M), Reformer   2,113
Cartwright (C), Tory   1,995
Knightley (K), Tory   1,401

Knightley said 'for his part he considered Parliamentary reform meant Parliamentary robbery'. Classification of Freeholders in respect to their rank and occupations, with the distribution of their votes to the several candidates:

No. of each	Rank and occupation	Althorp	Milton	Cartwright	Knightley
1	Earl	1	0	0	0
1	Lord	0	0	1	0
3	Honorables	1	1	2	2
6	Baronets	3	3	3	3
1	General in the Army	1	1	0	0
2	Colonels ditto	1	1	1	1
1	Major, R.N.	1	1	0	0
141	Esquires	54	43	92	80
374	Gentlemen	223	205	169	117
239	Clergymen	62	49	184	169
20	Dissenting ministers	19	20	0	0
42	Attorneys at Law and Solicitors	16	15	27	25
46	Doctors in Medicine, Surgeons, etc.	24	19	26	19
10	Bankers	7	6	4	2
9	Merchants	7	5	4	2
4	Ironfounders	4	4	0	0
14	Ironmongers	10	8	6	2
59	Drapers	45	41	17	12
78	Grocers	60	52	24	15
2	Tea dealers	2	2	0	0
3	Tallow chandlers	3	3	0	0
1	Cheesemonger	1	1	0	0
8	Druggists	5	4	4	3
23	Boot & Shoe manufacturers	23	21	1	0
3	Tanners	2	3	0	0
14	Curriers	13	12	2	1
4	Leather Factors, etc.	4	3	1	0
5	Feltmongers	5	3	2	0
7	Woolstaplers	5	6	1	0
4	Ribbon and Silk Manufacturers	4	4	0	0
5	Hosiers	3	3	2	2
1	Carpet Manufacturer	1	1	0	0

The Northamptonshire election of 1831 (cont.)

No. of each	Rank and occupation	Althorp	Milton	Cartwright	Knightley
5	Land Surveyors	2	2	3	3
7	Printers	3	3	4	4
8	Booksellers and Stationers	6	4	4	2
11	Common Brewers	5	4	7	6
12	Coal Merchants	8	5	7	4
1	Cloth Worker	1	1	0	0
3	Horse Dealers	1	1	1	1
3	Coach Builders	1	0	3	2
6	Lace Merchants	5	4	1	1
14	Timber Merchants	10	6	8	4
11	Builders	7	8	3	3
126	Carpenters	85	75	51	28
49	Bricklayers and Masons	30	22	23	13
22	Plumbers, Glaziers & Painters	14	11	11	5
51	Smiths	38	27	24	9
18	Slaters & Plasterers	6	4	14	9
7	Brickmakers	5	6	1	1
1	Lime-burner	1	1	0	0
7	Cabinetmakers	5	4	2	2
5	Upholsterers	3	1	4	2
15	Wine and Spirit Merchants	10	8	7	5
140	Innholders, Victuallers, etc.	88	79	58	37
39	Maltsters	28	17	21	9
117	Butchers	75	58	59	34
108	Bakers	67	60	46	36
5	Corn Dealers	3	2	3	1
58	Millers	45	35	20	11
2	Mealmen	1	2	0	1
1	Corn Meter	1	1	0	0
3	Millwrights	3	2	1	0
1,588	Agriculturalists	920	772	779	536
10	Auctioneers	9	9	1	1
67	Nurserymen and Gardeners	42	43	26	19
2	Seedsmen	1	1	1	1
9	Saddlers	5	4	4	4
6	Hatters	5	4	2	1
14	Collar & Harness Makers	9	8	6	5
15	Hairdressers and Perfumers	12	8	6	4
40	Tailors	25	26	12	12
2	Glovers and Breeches Makers	1	1	1	1

The Northamptonshire election of 1831 (cont.)

No. of each	Rank and occupation	Althorp	Milton	Cartwright	Knightley
7	Watchmakers	7	6	1	0
4	Confectioners	4	3	0	1
40	Wheelwrights	27	21	19	11
16	Coopers	12	11	5	3
3	Turners & Chairmakers	3	3	0	0
5	Basket & Mat Makers	4	3	2	1
5	Braziers & Tin-plate Workers	4	3	2	1
4	Fishmongers	3	2	2	1
8	Veterinary Surgeons	5	5	3	3
1	Paper Maker	0	1	0	0
1	Banker's Clerk	1	1	0	0
1	Artist	1	1	0	0
2	Pawnbrokers	2	2	0	0
2	Dyers	2	2	0	0
114	Shoemakers	89	88	28	14
16	Weavers	13	12	1	1
2	Woolcombers	1	2	0	0
5	Hawkers	2	4	2	0
20	Shopkeepers, etc.	16	12	8	4
2	Flax Dressers, etc.	2	2	0	0
2	Brush and Sieve Makers	2	2	0	0
1	Straw Manufacturer	1	1	0	0
1	Gunmaker	1	1	0	0
1	Whip Manufacturer	1	1	0	0
1	Saddle-tree Maker	1	1	0	0
1	Parchment Maker	0	1	0	1
1	Pattern Maker	1	1	0	0
1	Pipe maker	1	0	1	0
1	Tawer	0	0	1	1
5	Sawyers	2	1	4	2
11	Pig Jobbers	3	6	7	5
14	Common Carriers	9	9	4	4
1	Gaoler	1	0	1	0
1	Sheriff's Officer	1	0	1	0
1	Attorney's Clerk	0	0	1	0
4	Toll Collectors & Road Surveyors	3	3	1	1
65	Schoolmasters	21	13	53	31
1	Sailor	1	1	0	0
1	Ship Caulker	1	1	0	0
1	Coachman	0	0	1	0
17	Gamekeepers and Servants	8	7	9	9
1	Overseer	0	0	1	1
31	Parish Clerks	9	11	19	13
21	Beedsmen or Inmates of Almshouses	1	0	20	21

The Northamptonshire election of 1831 (cont.)

The votes of a few of the most prominent classes

	No.	Single votes				Double votes						Summary			
		A	M	C	K	A and M	A and C	A and K	M and C	M and K	C and K	A	M	C	K
The magistracy															
Laymen	27	1	—	—	—	4	3	—	—	—	19 ⎫	9	4	42	38
Clergy	20	—	—	—	—	—	1	—	—	—	19 ⎭				
The clergy	239	3	2	6	3	46	13	—	—	1	165	62	49	184	169
Solicitors etc.	42	—	—	1	—	15	1	—	—	—	25	16	15	27	25
Medical practitioners															
M.D.'s	10	—	—	—	—	4	—	—	—	—	6 ⎫	24	19	26	19
Surgeons, etc.	36	—	1	3	—	14	5	1	—	—	12 ⎭				
Agriculturalists, described as graziers, farmers and yeomen	1,588	39	32	88	10	714	164	3	15	11	512	920	772	779	536
Schoolmasters	65	1	2	10	—	10	11	—	1	—	31	21	13	53	31
Parish clerks	31	1	4	5	—	7	1	—	—	—	13	9	11	19	13

The Norwich election of 1830 (29–30 July)

The pollbook is in Manchester University Library. The pollbook used by Mr Brecknell is in Norwich City Library.

Result:	Grant, Whig	2,279
	Gurney, Whig	2,263*
	Peel, Tory	1,912
	Ogle, Tory	1,762
Splits:	Gurney and Grant	2,231
	Peel and Ogle	1,756

According to calculations made and kindly shown to me by Mr N. P. Brecknell, these groups voted as follows:

	For Gurney and Grant	For Peel and Ogle
Cordwainers	125	88
Manufacturers (textile)	50	22
Textile workers (silk and worsted weavers and wool combers)	310	137
'Freeholders' (various social positions and occupations)	362	276

In 1830 there were 4,202 freemen voters.

According to my own calculations, selected categories of 'in-voters' (residents) and 'out-voters' voted as follows:

In-voters				
Selected categories	Gurney	Grant	Peel	Ogle
Gentlemen	112	115	124	122
Bankers	2	2	1	1
Surgeons	6	6	11	11
Farmers	3	3	2	2
Lawyers	8	10	33	32
Merchants	23	23	11	10
Aldermen and Mayor	7	7	11	11
Architects	0	0	2	2
Servants, gardeners, etc.	31	31	39	35
Dissenting ministers	1	2	0	0
Brewers	8	7	6	5
Publicans	34	33	35	32
Tailors	56	54	47	43
Printers	7	8	14	14
Butchers	20	20	14	14
Grocers	44	44	25	24
Watermen	29	26	19	18
Labourers	10	7	23	21
Out-voters				
Gentlemen	87	85	72	68
Farmers	71	71	33	32
Merchants	14	15	7	7
Officers	0	0	11	10
Lawyers	7	4	14	10
Labourers	9	9	5	4

None of the subsequent pollbooks for Norwich elections stated voters' occupations.

* Henry Stooks Smith gives Gurney 2,363 votes.

The Nottingham Borough election of 1852

The pollbook is in the Guildhall Library.

Result: Rt. Hon. Edward Strutt, Liberal   1,960
John Walter, Conservative   1,863
Charles Sturgeon, Chartist   512

Selected categories	Sturgeon	Strutt	Walter
Lace manufacturers	4	114	52
Labourers	12	9	29
Surgeons	0	12	13
Merchants	1	7	8
Police	0	3	1
Ironfounders	0	5	1
Postmaster	0	0	1
Ministers	0	5	2
Railwaymen	0	3	1
Bankers	0	3	4
Coalmaster	0	1	0
Clergy	0	1	1

The Nottinghamshire (South) election of 1846

The pollbook is in the Guildhall Library. It does not state the occupations of voters. The by-election was caused by the acceptance of office by the Earl of Lincoln; the issue was Free Trade in corn, raised by the 'Nottinghamshire Agricultural Protection Society', who brought forward T. B. Hildyard of Flintham Hall, Notts.

Result: T. B. Hildyard, Conservative   1,736
Lord Lincoln, Peelite   1,049

	Lincoln	Hildyard
Clergy	21	29

The Oldham election of 1832

The pollbook is in Oldham Public Library.

The following table gives an analysis of the small Tory and Whig minority in the first election ever held at Oldham, 1832. The popular party (those voting for the successful candidates Fielden and Cobbett) have not been analysed.

	Bright (Whig)	Burge (Tory)
Gentlemen	11	8
Surgeons	2	0
Solicitors	3	0
Clergymen	1	3
Auctioneers, surveyors, etc.	4	4
Farmers	16	12
Innkeepers	1	1
Clerks	5	3
Butchers	4	2
Other shopkeepers	12	8
Building and metal craftsmen	10	9

The Oldham election of 1832 (cont.)

	Bright (Whig)	Burge (Tory)
Corn, timber, coal and waste dealers	9	2
Hat manufacturers	16	2
Cotton manufacturers	6	2
Machine makers	3	0
Cotton spinners	28	12
Other operatives	4	2
Coal master	0	1
Colliers	0	2
Miscellaneous	15	13

The Oldham election of 1847

Oldham Public Library has pollbooks giving occupations for 1832, 1852, 1865 and for the 1852 by-election. The 1847 pollbook, though not giving occupations, contains these remarks in its preface:

'We the Committee of Working Men beg to call the especial attention of the Factory Workers and the Public of Oldham to this Fact, that nearly all the Mill Owners and Manufacturers (about 200) in the Borough voted against Mr Fielden, a significant proof as to whether it was "Dictation" or the Ten Hours Bill which has called forth their vengeance.

The attention of the Industrious Classes and Public of this Borough is also drawn to the conduct of the Religious, Dissenting, and Nonconforming part of the Electors, in splitting their votes between Fox and Duncuft, one of whom, as a Churchman...' [etc.]

There follows a list of employers who voted against Fielden. Of these, some 98, marked with an asterisk, were subscribers to the Anti-Corn Law League.

The Oldham election of July 1852

The pollbook is in Oldham Public Library.

Result: Cobbett, Conservative 957
Duncuft, Conservative 868
Fox, Liberal 777

Selected categories*	Duncuft and Cobbett	Cobbett and Fox	Duncuft and Fox	Fox	Cobbett	Duncuft
Agents and foremen	5	0	6	41	6	4
Cotton waste dealers	9	0	2	30	0	0
Spinners and manufacturers	40	9	35	187	13	30
Farmers	141	26	12	15	7	3
Beersellers	89	20	6	13	16	1
Innkeepers	83	20	2	13	10	7
Shopkeepers	172	35	51	149	28	14
Clergy, gentry, professional	88	0	0	63	0	18

* About 100 votes are not listed in the table as the occupation of those giving them was either not stated in the pollbook, or it fell outside the main categories.

The Oldham by-election of 1852

The pollbook is in Oldham Public Library.

Result: Fox, Liberal   895
Heald, Conservative 783

All voters	Fox	Heald
Gentry, clergy, professional	79	99
Innkeepers	42	86
Beersellers	32	109
Farmers	70	174
Cotton spinners, manufacturers, and other employers	214	75
Grocers	96	87
Tailors and drapers	44	11
Butchers	9	28
Other shopkeepers	116	62
Shoemakers, cloggers	22	13
Unclassified and miscellaneous	69	53

The Oldham election of 1865

The pollbook is in Oldham Public Library.

Result: Hibbert, Liberal   1,105
Platt, Liberal   1,076
Cobbett, Conservative   898
Spinks, Conservative   845

Of these: For Cobbett and Spinks   800
For Hibbert and Platt   1,031

Only these latter 'straight party votes' are analysed below.*

Selected categories	Liberal	Conservative
I. Gentlemen	7	34
Anglican clergy	0	8
Dissenting ministers	3	0
Solicitors	4	7
Surgeons	5	5
R.C. priest	1	0
Auctioneers	3	0
Architects	4	1
Schoolmasters	4	2
Surveyors	0	2
Organist	0	1
Governor of workhouse	0	1
II. Innkeepers	41	80
Beersellers	30	74
Brewer	0	1
Farmers	38	111

* A multitude of minor occupations and many voters whose occupations were not given are not listed.

The Oldham election of 1865 (cont.)

Selected categories	Liberal	Conservative
III. Colliery owner	3	2
Collier	1	0
Colliery manager	0	1
Colliery overlooker	0	1
IV. Grocers	34	46
Butchers	12	20
Pawnbrokers	4	3
Druggist	9	5
Other shopkeepers	76	40
V. Engine-driver	3	1
Stationmaster	1	0
VI. Cotton spinners	156	44
Cotton manufacturers	1	7
Cotton waste dealers	34	13
Managers	12	3
VII. Clerks	15	4
Mechanics	35	4
Shoemakers, cloggers	19	9
Tailors	8	2
Ironfounders	6	1
Timber dealers	5	0

The Oxford City election of 1835

The pollbook is in the Bodleian Library.

Result: W. H. Hughes, Conservative   1,394
D. Maclean, Conservative   1,217
T. Stonor, Liberal   1,022

Selected categories	Stonor	Hughes	Maclean
Servants	8	28	30
Policemen	3	4	4
Surgeons	0	1	3
Dissenting ministers	1	1	1
Governor of gaol	0	1	1
R.C. priest	1	1	0
College servants	8	120	153
Doctors of Divinity	0	0	3
Doctors of Law	0	0	1
Bedels	0	2	4
Professors	1	1	4
Manciples	0	1	2
Parish clerks	1	3	5
Organists	0	1	2
Anglican clergy	0	5	11
University Marshal	0	0	1

The Oxford City election of 1841

The pollbook is in the Bodleian Library.

Result: Langston, Liberal   1,349
Maclean, Conservative   1,238
Malcolm, Conservative   1,031

Freemen: selected categories	Langston	Maclean	Malcolm
Carpenters	48	17	9
Tailors	103	76	59
Butchers	25	21	13
Gentlemen	26	36	32
Victuallers	12	3	3
Wine merchants	5	5	5
Shoemakers	67	50	40
Labourers	21	16	12
Servants	4	9	9
Lawyers	4	8	9
Saddlers	7	5	4
Farmers	6	15	17
Grocers	9	13	12
College servants	0	12	11
Surgeons	0	4	4
Bankers	0	4	4

£10 Householders: selected categories	Langston	Maclean	Malcolm
Labourers	17	13	7
Butchers	18	8	6
Tailors	50	23	17
Servants	15	71	69
College servants	7	68	67
Victuallers	45	34	26
Lawyers	4	5	3
Shoemakers	35	19	14
Grocers	15	7	5
Carpenters	50	24	15
Saddlers	4	2	0
Gentlemen	29	28	23
Surgeons	2	10	8
Police	1	5	4
Dissenting ministers	2	1	1
Farmers	0	2	2
Banker	1	0	0
Organists	0	3	3

The Peterborough elections of 1852

From the report on the Peterborough election, *Parl. Papers* 1852–3, XVII, 623. In 1852 Peterborough had 532 electors, nearly half of whom were tenants of Earl Fitzwilliam. 432 out of 532 were £10 householders. Of the £10 householders who were tenants of the Earl, there voted as follows:

July 1852	Fitzwilliam (Liberal)	Watson (Liberal)	Clifton (Conservative)
Plumps	2	4	20
Splits	113	113	—
Splits	12	—	12
Splits	—	2	2
	127	119	34

December 1852*

Sir G. C. Lewis (Liberal)	110
Whalley (Independent, against Fitzwilliam)	38

The point brought out here is that, even when there was no great issue at stake, and even when aristocratic influence was supported, as in this case, by disguised evictions and loss of custom, a sizeable minority of urban tenants would vote against what they thought were the wishes of their landlords.

* McCalmont gives the overall result as Lewis 218, Whalley 233.

The Preston election of 8 December 1830

The pollbook, which is in Manchester Public Library, takes the form of a single alphabetical list of 7,122 voters. Only those whose names began with A and B are analysed below.

Result: Henry Hunt	3,730	
Rt. Hon. E. G. Stanley	3,392	

Voters A and B only	Stanley	Hunt
I. The upper crust		
Gentlemen	27	1
Lawyers	5	0
Surgeons	3	0
II. Business and dependants		
Innkeepers	10	0
Schoolmasters	9	0
Commercial and clerical	15	6
Sexton	1	0
Yeoman	0	1
Builders	2	0
Cheese, flour, corn dealers	6	0
Timber merchant	1	0
Millers	5	5
Coal dealers	3	3
Brewers	2	7
Others*	2	3

* Coachmaker, pipemaker, blacking maker, malt crusher.

The Preston election of 8 December 1830 (cont.)

Voters A and B only	Stanley	Hunt
III. Retailers		
Butchers	4	0
Booksellers	0	2
Other shopkeepers	42	13
IV. Unskilled, servants, etc.		
Miscellaneous*	16	9
Servants, etc.†	22	1
Lamplighters	3	0
Constables	2	0
Boatmen	3	0
Porters	3	1
Rag gatherers	1	5
Carters	17	3
Labourers	32	35
V. Textiles		
Flax dressers	2	2
Warehousemen	9	0
Overlookers	3	2
Engine tenders	6	0
Cotton manufacturers	3	0
Calico printer	1	1
Sizers	3	2
Dressers	6	1
Carders	6	3
Warpers	19	8
Spinners	24	56
Weavers	28	172
Other operatives‡	5	9
Mechanics	16	36
Reed, roller, shuttle, spindle makers	1	6
VI. Craftsmen		
Shoemakers, cloggers	15	25
Tailors	4	14
Sawyers	5	8
Smith, blacksmith	4	8
Tin, brass, tinplate, silver; watch-makers and gunsmiths	12	3
Moulder, ironfounder	4	6
Bricklayer, plasterer, mason, painter, slater	10	6
Printers	6	2
Grinder, screwmaker, nailor, foundryman, filecutter	2	8
Chair, brush, basket, and cabinet-maker, turner, upholsterer	10	11

* Sweep, town crier, hawker, farrier, horsebreaker, discharger, waterman, bailiff, postboy, turnkey, watchman, horsekeeper, jobber, horsetender, scavenger, pavior, husbandman.

† Servants, coachmen, gardeners, grooms, ostlers, waiters.

‡ Rover, drawer-in, twister, stripper, stretcher.

The Preston election of 8 December 1830 (cont.)

	Stanley	Hunt
VI. Craftsmen (*cont.*)		
Joiners, carpenters	18	22
Saddlers	4	1
Plumbers	4	0
Tanner, currier, skinner	4	5
Potter	0	2
Others*	6	2

* Umbrella and staymaker, bookbinder, cooper, roper.

The Preston election of 1841

The pollbook is in Manchester Public Library.

Result: Sir Hesketh Fleetwood, Liberal   1,655
Sir George Strickland, Liberal   1,629
R. Townley Parker, Conservative   1,270
Charles Swainson, Conservative   1,255

Selected categories only:

	Fleetwood	Strickland	Parker	Swainson
I. Respectables and dependants				
Gentlemen	24	22	40	40
Surgeons	5	4	11	10
Attorneys	13	13	41	41
Anglican clergy	0	0	4	4
Parish clerk	0	0	1	1
Bankers	3	3	6	6
Manufacturers	10	10	11	11
Turnkeys	0	0	2	2
Constable	0	0	1	1
Ministers	3	4	0	0
Auctioneers	3	2	4	3
II. Trade				
Innkeepers	27	27	26	26
Beersellers	6	6	0	0
Butchers	14	15	20	21
Farmers	2	1	7	7
III. Labour				
Tailors	40	37	22	21
Shoemakers	83	81	30	30
Cloggers	13	13	0	0
Overlookers	25	25	36	35
Spinners	112	112	89	89
Weavers	261	260	90	93

The Preston election of 1852

This analysis is based on a pollbook in Manchester Public Library. A note at the end explains, 'When the Elector is registered through a £10 Qualification, his Profession or Business is not given.' As most electors were qualified as £10 householders, the analysis below creates no presumption as to the general

The Preston election of 1852 (cont.)

voting pattern except for occupations like weavers and spinners who were unlikely to be qualified except as freemen.

Result: Robert Townley Parker, Conservative   1,335
Sir George Strickland, Bt., Radical   1,253
C. P. Grenfell, Whig   1,127
James German, Radical   692

Freemen voters only:

selected categories	Strickland	German	Grenfell	Parker
Manufacturers	2	1	0	1
Overlookers	18	5	13	12
Weavers	137	64	90	44
Spinners	45	18	30	36
Innkeepers	3	0	2	5
Brewers	3	3	0	0
Beersellers	2	1	1	0
Butchers	5	6	7	10
Shoemakers	38	21	22	24
Tailors	15	12	8	8
Gentlemen	2	1	2	2
Banker	0	0	0	1
Anglican clergy	0	0	1	1
Minister	1	0	1	0
Medical, legal, auctioneer	0	0	0	3

Parker's vote		Strickland's vote		Grenfell's vote	
Plumps	358	Plumps	364	Plumps	75
and Strickland	101	and Grenfell	396	and Parker	621
and Grenfell	621	and German	392	and Strickland	396
and German	255	and Parker	101	and German	35

German's vote

Plumps	10
and Strickland	392
and Parker	255
and Grenfell	35

The religious atmosphere of this election is shown in the following quotation
from a contemporary broadsheet bound together with the 1852 pollbook:

Popery—No Never

(Tune: 'Hearts of Oak')

verse 2   The vile priests of Rome would enslave us we know,
A wily, a base, an insidious foe:
They would make Britain's sons their base ignorant slaves,
As they have in each Land that their tyranny braves.
Church and Queen is our cause,
Firm and staunch are our men,
Then PARKER FOR EVER
Popery—no never.
We'll vote, as did our Fathers vote,
Again and again.

The Preston election of 1852 (cont.)

verse 3   The women of England so dear to these isles,
Shall mark all our acts, and reward with their smiles.
As they see us defending the land of their birth,
Old Protestant England—the pride of the Earth.
Church and Queen is our cause,
Firm and staunch are our men,
Then Grenfell FOR EVER
Popery—no never...[etc.]

The Reading election of 1837

The pollbook is in the Guildhall Library.

Result: Talford, Liberal   468
Palmer, Liberal   457
Russell, Conservative   448

Selected categories	Talford	Palmer	Russell
Surgeons	5	5	7
Clergy	0	0	7
Shoemakers	6	6	3
Dissenting ministers	4	4	0
Organist	1	1	0
Mayor	1	1	0
Parish clerk	0	0	1
Chymists	2	2	3
Biscuit maker	1	0	0
R.C. priest	1	1	0
Police	1	1	0
Manufacturer	1	1	0

The Reading election of 1841

The pollbook is in the Guildhall Library.

Result: Charles Russell, Conservative   576
Viscount Chelsea, Conservative   564
Thomas Mills, Liberal   409
Wm. Tooke, Liberal   396

Selected categories	Mills	Tooke	Russell	Chelsea
Surgeons	3	3	12	11
Butchers	6	6	6	6
Grocers	23	23	20	19
Shoemakers	26	25	16	15
Labourers	3	3	1	1
Clergy	0	0	10	10
Parish clerk	0	0	1	1
Railwayman	0	0	1	1
Police	0	0	1	1
Farmers	3	2	2	2
Dissenting ministers	2	2	1	1
Engineers	1	1	1	1
Biscuit baker	1	1	0	0
Umbrella makers	3	3	0	0

The Rochdale election of 1841

The pollbook is in Rochdale Public Library.

Result:* W. S. Crawford, Radical   399
Fenton, Conservative   335

	Radical	Con-servative		Radical	Con-servative
I. Drink interest			Butchers	14	11
Beersellers	28	24	Clockmakers	2	2
Publicans	14	31	Cloggers	4	2
Others	5	4	Confectioners	0	3
	47	59	Curriers	5	2
			Drapers	21	4
II. Textile interest			Druggists	4	4
Weavers	24	9	Earthenware	1	0
Woolsorters	3	5	Fishmonger	0	1
Woolstaplers	16	5	Greengrocers	3	0
Machinery	7	3	Grocers	58	22
makers			Hatters	7	2
Overlookers	1	5	Ironmongers	1	2
Shoddy dealers	0	6	Pawnbrokers	3	3
Dyers	5	1	Saddlers	2	1
Cotton masters	19	13	Tailors	9	6
Cotton sheet	1	1	Tallow sellers	1	1
makers			Tripe seller	0	1
Fustian dresser	0	1	Watermen	2	0
Manufacturers	26	16		154	73
	102	65	**V. Respectables and**		
III. Craftsmen			**dependants**		
Blacksmiths	3	3	Agents	4	3
Blacking maker	1	0	Auctioneers	1	3
Bricklayers	2	1	Bailiffs	0	7
Brush maker	0	1	Bankers	0	4
Coachmaker	1	0	Brokers	1	4
Engineers	3	1	Carriers	3	2
File cutters	0	1	Cheese factor	1	0
Ironfounders	6	5	Clerks	5	8
Machine	9	1	Commercial	1	0
makers			traveller		
Masons	0	3	Corn and malt	6	2
Nail maker	1	1	Farmers	1	5
Plumbers	3	4	Gardeners	1	3
Printers	3	2	Gentlemen	6	22
Ropers	2	2	Ministers	1	2
Tinplate makers	5	2	Organists,	0	4
Wheelwrights	3	1	sextons		
Whitesmiths	2	0	Schoolmasters	5	3
	44	28	Solicitors	5	14
IV. Retailers			Surgeons	4	4
Barbers	6	3	Surveyor	0	1
Shoemakers	11	3	Servants, etc.	2	8
				47	99

* McCalmont's figure of 338 for Fenton and 339 for Crawford does not accord with the pollbook or with Bean.

M

The Rochdale election of 1857

The pollbook is in the Rochdale Public Library.

Result: Ramsay, Conservative   529
        Miall, Liberal   487

	Liberal	Conservative			Liberal	Conservative
I. Drink				Warehousemen	4	2
Beersellers	16	63		Waste dealers	6	11
Publicans	10	46		Dentists	2	0
Wine dealers	1	5		Flannel dealers	2	1
Spirits dealer	0	1		Wool staplers	13	6
Maltster	0	1			87	98
Hop merchant	0	1				
Brewer	0	1		**V. Craftsmen**		
Cooper	1	0		Blacksmiths	3	3
	28	118		Boilermakers	3	1
II. Capital				Shoemakers	13	5
Bankers	0	3		Brass, iron	6	5
Woollen manu-	18	22		founders		
facturers				Bricksetters	3	1
Corn millers	1	2		Brushmakers	1	2
Cotton spinners	12	26		Cabinet makers	8	3
Dyers	3	1		Coachbuilders	6	9
	34	54		Cardmakers	2	0
III. Retailers				Cloggers	4	9
Confectioners	2	2		Machine makers	11	4
Drapers	35	8		Mechanics	5	1
Druggists	3	7		Painters	5	3
Earthenware	1	1		Plumbers	1	5
Greengrocers	4	0		Reed makers	4	2
Grocers	71	37		Ropers	1	1
Hairdressers	7	7		Saddlers	0	3
Hatters	5	1		Shuttle makers	3	0
Ironmongers	4	1		Spindle makers	0	2
Pawnbrokers	4	1		Stone masons	0	3
Smallware	7	4		Tailors	11	6
Tallow sellers	0	2		Tinners	2	3
Bakers	1	1		Watch makers	3	2
Booksellers	7	5		Weavers	3	5
Butchers	16	25		Wool sorters	8	2
	167	102		Curriers	4	1
IV. Respectables,				Engineers	9	7
merchants				Doffing Plate	3	0
Agents	29	31		makers		
Attorneys	2	13		Joiners	11	7
Auctioneers	2	2			133	95
Brokers	1	2		**VI. Others**		
Cheese factors	2	2		Labourers	3	2
Managers	6	6		Farmers	0	4
Ministers	13	5		Gardeners	0	3
Schoolmasters	2	4		Carriers	1	4
Surgeons	2	11		Miscellaneous	33	49
Surveyors	1	2			37	62

The Rochester election of August 1830

The pollbook is in the Institute of Historical Research.

Result: Ralph Bernal, Whig   429
Viscount Villiers, Tory   417
John Mills, Tory   339

Selected categories	Bernal	Villiers	Mills
Gentlemen	52	56	22
Officers	3	3	0
Surgeons	7	8	2
Solicitors	3	6	2
Farmers	4	4	2
Victuallers	16	11	12
Grocers	5	6	9
Chemists	4	1	0
Tailors	15	7	14
Cordwainers	17	12	27
Labourers	7	9	10
Shipwrights	17	18	30
Pilots	3	3	1
Mariners	23	30	15
Dredgermen	26	22	39
Cabinetmakers	10	8	6

Plumps		Splits	
Bernal	84	Bernal and Villiers	305
Villiers	50	Bernal and Mills	40
Mills	237	Villiers and Mills	62

Residences of voters at this election

Rochester	283
Strood	45
Gillingham	22
Chatham	67
Rest of Kent	161
London	178
Rest of England	23

The Rochester election of 1835

The pollbook is in the Guildhall Library.

Result: Ralph Bernal, Liberal   502
T. T. Hodges, Liberal   443
Lord Chas. Wellesley, Conservative   442

Selected categories	Bernal	Hodges	Wellesley
Shoemakers	25	23	29
Tailors	15	13	15
Fishermen	16	13	14
Dredgermen	27	25	21
Mariners	18	15	11
Saddlers	6	6	2

The Rochester election of 1835 (cont.)

Selected categories	Bernal	Hodges	Wellesley
Butchers	20	19	11
Grocers	20	18	12
Labourers	6	3	7
Surgeons	7	6	3
Victuallers	38	33	19
Gentlemen	54	49	49
Shipwrights	2	4	22
Pilots	2	1	1
Mayor	0	0	1
Serjeant at mace	0	0	1
Organist	0	0	1
Shipbuilders	1	1	0
Anglican clergy	3	2	13
Common councilmen	2	2	5
Aldermen	3	3	5
Verger	0	0	1
Farmers	7	6	10
Gaoler	0	0	1
Bankers	2	2	0
Police	0	0	1
Officers	0	0	5
Town clerk	0	0	1
Barge owner	1	1	0

The Rochester election of 1852

The pollbook is in the Guildhall Library.

Result: Villiers, Conservative   599
Maddock, Conservative   594
Bernal, Liberal   515
Twisden Hodges, Liberal   509

Selected categories	Bernal	Hodges	Villiers	Maddock
Officers	3	2	5	5
Town Crier	0	0	1	1
Police	0	0	9	9
Farmers	1	1	11	11
Verger	0	0	1	1
Dredgermen	6	7	14	15
Bargemen	6	6	3	3
Pilots	1	0	1	1
Ship owners	2	2	0	0
Relieving officer	1	1	0	0
Parish clerks	0	0	2	2
Watermen	1	1	3	3
Sailmakers	3	4	5	6
Inspector of weights	0	0	1	1
Organist	0	0	1	1
Dissenting minister	1	1	0	0

The Rochester election of 1852 (cont.)

Selected categories	Bernal	Hodges	Villiers	Maddock
Shipwrights	6	5	11	11
Shipbuilder	1	1	0	0
Clergy	1	1	3	3
Surgeons	4	4	5	6
Shoemakers	28	28	23	23
Tailors	10	10	10	10
Fishermen	11	9	16	14
Mariners	32	31	45	44
Butchers	11	11	17	17
Grocers	22	22	12	12
Labourers	18	18	17	17
Victuallers	25	25	17	17
Gentlemen	42	42	43	43

The Rochester election of 1856

The pollbook is in the Guildhall Library.

Result: Wykeham Martin, Liberal 560
Henry Bodkin, Conservative 499

Selected categories	Martin	Bodkin
Macebearers	0	2
Bankers	0	2
Relieving officers	1	1
Railwaymen	2	1
Parish clerk	1	0
Engineers	4	0
Officers	1	4
Pilot	0	1
Farmers	5	11
Police	0	14
Bargemen	14	5
Organist	0	1
Dredgermen	9	10
Inspector of weights	0	1
Town crier	0	1
Shipwrights	6	13
Clergy	1	2
Saddlers	1	3
Fishermen	4	9
Shoemakers	29	17
Tailors	10	10
Mariners	35	23
Butchers	14	13
Grocers	19	9
Labourers	19	23
Surgeons	10	4
Gentlemen	47	32
Shipowners	2	0

The Rochester election of 1859

The pollbook is in the Guildhall Library.

Result: Wykeham Martin, Liberal   665
Kinglake, Liberal   662
Money, Conservative   505
Mitchell, Conservative   492

Selected categories	Martin	Kinglake	Money	Mitchell
Shoemakers	23	22	18	17
Fishermen	1	1	3	3
Mariners	33	31	21	21
Clergy	2	2	7	7
Dissenting ministers	2	2	0	0
Parish clerk	0	0	1	1
Organist	0	0	1	1
Labourers	16	16	18	18
Surgeons	9	9	9	9
Railwaymen	2	2	1	1
Officers	1	1	1	1
Shipowners	4	4	0	0
Shipwrights	7	7	13	13
Pilots	1	1	1	1
Dredgermen	22	21	23	22
Farmers	2	2	11	15
Barge builder	1	1	0	0
Barge owners	2	2	1	1
Bargemen	20	16	0	0
Sanitary inspector	0	0	1	1
Macebearers	0	0	2	2
Relieving officer	1	1	0	0
Engineers	3	3	2	2
Vergers	0	0	2	2
Town crier	0	0	1	1
Police	0	0	2	2

The Rochester election of 1865

The pollbook is in the Guildhall Library.

Result: Wykeham Martin, Liberal   855
Kinglake, Liberal   792
Smee, Conservative   414

Selected categories	Martin	Kinglake	Smee
Shoemakers	19	17	11
Fishermen	4	3	5
Mariners	39	38	17
Clergy	2	2	3
Dissenting ministers	1	1	0
Parish clerks	1	1	1

The Rochester election of 1865 (cont.)

Selected categories	Martin	Kinglake	Smee
Labourers	23	18	16
Surgeons	8	7	1
Railwaymen	13	13	1
Officers	3	3	1
Shipwrights	7	6	7
Ship owner	1	1	0
Dredgermen	15	13	3
Farmers	1	1	9
Barge owners	2	2	0
Bargemen	7	4	8
Bargemasters	21	21	7
Engineers	9	9	1
Verger	0	0	1
Macebearer	1	1	0

The Rochester election of 1868

The pollbook is in the Institute of Historical Research.

Result: P. W. Martin, Liberal   1,458
J. A. Kinglake, Liberal   1,305
A. Smee, Conservative   703

Selected categories	Martin	Smee
Anglican clergy	0	4
Vergers	0	3
Organist	0	1
Presbyterian minister	1	0
Publicans	33	17
Brewers	2	2
Beersellers	11	8
Labourers	180	116
Shoemakers	25	12
Surgeons	5	4
Gentlemen	59	21
Pensioners	6	8
Engineers	6	0
Postmen	8	1
Saddlers	2	0
Postmaster	0	1
Turnkeys	9	5
Customs	4	1
Coastguard	2	0
Wharfingers	5	1
Master mariners	14	0
Mariners	40	21
Sailmakers	12	8
Fishermen	24	14

The Rochester election of 1868 (cont.)

Selected categories	Martin	Smee
Shipwrights	27	19
Watermen	10	6
Dredgermen	9	3
Coalwhippers	1	5
Bargemasters and owners	41	2
Bargebuilder	1	0
Bargemen	7	36

The Rutland election of 1841

The pollbook is in Cambridge University Library.

Result: G. J. Heathcote, Liberal	767
Hon. W. H. Dawnay, Conservative	676
Hon. C. G. Noel, Liberal	664

	Noel	Heathcote	Dawnay	Abstained
Clergymen	9	19	39	8

The Sandwich election of May 1831

The pollbook is in the Institute of Historical Research.

Result: Joseph Marryat, Whig	498
Sir E. T. Troubridge, Whig	397
S. G. Price, Tory	297

Selected categories	Marryat	Troubridge	Price
Gentlemen	43	36	30
Officers	4	15	4
Surgeons	1	3	1
Sextons	2	1	1
Pilots	3	1	2
Innkeepers	10	6	6
Butchers	7	5	4
Grocers	11	9	6
Carpenters	29	26	11
Cabinetmakers	15	10	7
Labourers	56	23	39
Mariners	36	35	12
Tailors	17	13	9
Shoemakers	24	15	13
Weavers	4	4	1
Farmers	16	17	2

Plumps		Splits	
Marryat	20	Marryat and Price	156
Troubridge	61	Price and Troubridge	14
Price	127	Troubridge and Marryat	322

The Sandwich election of 1852

The pollbook is in the Guildhall Library.

Result: Pelham Clinton, Peelite   460
French, Liberal   257

Selected categories	French	Clinton
Pilots	1	45
Officers	5	6
Clergy	0	5
Surgeons	3	5
Mariners	4	24
Butchers	2	15
Grocers	13	9
Dissenting ministers	4	0
Shoemakers	9	14
Labourers	2	21
Master of the hospital	0	1

The Sandwich election of 1859

The pollbook is in the Guildhall Library.

Result: Hugessen, Liberal   497
Paget, Liberal   458
Fergusson, Conservative   404
Lewis, Conservative   328

Selected categories	Hugessen	Paget	Fergusson	Lewis
Pilots	26	24	11	7
Officers	5	6	6	6
Clergy	0	0	5	5
Surgeons	7	6	5	4
Mariners	14	15	11	11
Butchers	10	11	14	9
Grocers	21	21	8	8
Dissenting ministers	5	6	1	1
Shoemakers	10	10	6	6
Labourers	14	11	19	17
Hospitalians	6	7	1	0
Farmers	8	10	7	6
Engineer	0	0	1	1
Railwayman	1	0	1	0
Fishermen	0	0	2	2
Gasworkers	2	2	1	1

The Sandwich, Deal, and Walmer election of 1868

The pollbook is in the Guildhall Library.

Result: E. H. Knatchbull-Hugessen, Liberal   933
H. A. Brassey, Liberal   923
Henry Worms, Conservative   710

Selected categories	Hugessen	Brassey	Worms
Officers	2	0	5
Coastguards	6	6	13
Clergymen	4	1	11
Dissenting ministers	4	4	0
Sexton	1	1	0
R.C. priest	1	1	0
Brewers	6	6	1
Railwaymen	7	5	3
Surgeons	7	7	3
Lawyers	2	1	3
Farmers	16	17	10
Hospitalians	12	11	1
Butchers	10	11	21
Grocers	22	22	12
Victuallers	46	45	48
Beersellers	2	2	4
Shoemakers	35	31	15
Carpenters	33	32	21
Mariners	134	133	60
Labourers	119	128	102
Sweeps	5	5	0
Gentlemen	72	68	53
Pilots	34	33	20
Harbour master	0	0	1

The Scottish Universities election of 1868

G. W. T. Omond, in his book *The Lord Advocates of Scotland 1834–1880*, printed on page 245 an analysis of the voting of the ministers and clergy of the various denominations in the Scottish Universities election of 1868, when Playfair and Moncreiff were elected.

	Liberal	Tory
Established Church	67	1,221
Free Church	607	33
United Presbyterian	474	1
Episcopalians	4	78
Not classified	360	35
	1,512	1,368

If correct, these results are striking: but unfortunately no source is stated. Omond adds that a majority of the doctors in the constituency voted Liberal, and a majority of the lawyers were Tory.

The Shrewsbury election of August 1830

The pollbook is in the Institute of Historical Research.

Result: Richard Jenkins, Tory   754
R. A. Slaney, Whig   563
Panton Corbett, Tory   446

Selected categories	Slaney	Jenkins	Corbett
Parish clerks	0	2	2
Organist	0	1	0
Gentlemen	12	25	24
Bankers	2	2	5
Surgeons	3	6	7
Lawyers	0	7	8
Farmers	2	1	1
Innkeepers	8	12	6
Butchers	35	60	31
Grocers	12	14	15
Shoemakers	112	100	28
Weavers	9	5	2
Labourers	28	32	13

Splits		Plumps	
Jenkins and Slaney	362	Slaney	131
Jenkins and Corbett	357	Jenkins	35
Slaney and Corbett	70	Corbett	70

The Shrewsbury election of 1837

The pollbook is in the Institute of Historical Research.

Result: Jenkins, Conservative   700
Slaney, Liberal   697
Pelham, Conservative   655
Dashwood, Liberal   537

Selected categories	Slaney	Dashwood	Jenkins	Pelham
Gentlemen	26	18	49	46
Dissenting ministers	3	3	0	0
Parish clerks	0	0	2	2
Organist	0	0	1	1
Policeman	1	1	0	0
Gaoler	1	1	0	0
Bankers	1	0	4	4
Surgeons	3	1	10	12
Lawyers	6	5	19	21
Farmers	4	2	4	4
Publicans	39	27	25	26
Beersellers	6	6	5	5

The Shrewsbury election of 1837 (cont.)

Selected categories	Slaney	Dashwood	Jenkins	Pelham
Grocers	19	15	18	17
Butchers	27	20	28	26
Shoemakers	64	62	40	39
Carpenters	16	15	23	21
Tailors	37	29	37	31
Weavers	6	6	2	2
Curriers	6	6	4	4
Labourers	19	17	16	15

Splits

Jenkins and Pelham	604
Slaney and Dashwood	536

The Shrewsbury election of 1847

Result: E. H. Baldock, Protectionist 769
R. A. Slaney, Liberal   743
G. Tomline, Liberal   740

Selected categories	Tomline	Slaney	Baldock
Gentlemen	28	51	42
Surgeons	7	6	8
Solicitors	24	10	22
Bankers	3	1	3
Architects	2	0	2
Headmaster*	0	1	0
Brewers	1	4	3
Innkeepers	35	31	31
Beersellers	8	7	7
Grocers	8	20	12
Butchers	37	21	35
Organists	2	1	3
Vestry clerks	1	1	2
Turnkey	0	1	1
R.C. priest	1	1	0
Sweep	1	1	0
Police officers	4	0	4
Dissenting minister	0	1	0

* Dr Kennedy, D.D., of Shrewsbury School.

The Shrewsbury election of 1857

The pollbook is in Manchester Reference Library, as political tract P. 2759. Mr John Kenyon of Toronto University kindly drew my attention to this item.

Result: Tomline, Liberal	706
Slaney, Liberal	695
Huddleston, Conservative	548
Phibbs, Conservative	484

Twenty-six freeholders and 100 householders did not vote. Twenty-two voters plumped for one candidate, and 75 gave a vote for one Whig and one Tory

The Shrewsbury election of 1857 (cont.)

candidate. The following analysis, however, includes only those who gave a straight party vote for two candidates. Unfortunately, about 200 of these, or about one-sixth of those voting, had no occupation stated. The following figures must therefore be treated with caution

	Liberal	Conservative
I. Gentlemen	31	37
Clergy, teachers	8	2
Solicitors	11	17
Medical	4	13
Merchants	21	8
Masters	8	9
Professional, etc.	1	9
Clerks	22	29
Innkeepers	53	32
Farmers	4	0
II. Butchers	10	21
Other shopkeepers	106	51
Bakers, confectioners	20	2
Grocers	36	10
Mercers, drapers	17	7
Hatters	1	5
Chemists	5	5
Cowkeepers	7	6
Ironmongers	8	6
Stationers	2	2
Fishmongers	0	2
Barbers	6	4
Wine merchants	2	2
Jewellers	2	0
Painters	17	12
III. Printing crafts	12	13
Smiths, metal workers	20	23
Luxury crafts	8	12
Building crafts	42	30
Tailors	25	18
Shoemakers	40	19
Furniture makers	10	7
Other trades	21	14
IV. Engine-drivers	3	0
Engineers	18	0
V. Unskilled	23	21
VI. Occupation unstated	133	70

Summary:

	Liberal	Conservative
I. Commercial, professional, and property owning	155	156
II. Retailers	116	72
III. Craftsmen	195	136
IV. Engineers, engine-drivers	21	0
V. Unskilled	23	21
VI. Occupations unstated	133	70

The Shrewsbury election of 1868

The pollbook is in the Bodleian Library.

Result: Wm. J. Clement, Liberal 1,840
Jas. Figgins, Conservative 1,751
Robt. Crawford, Liberal 685

Figgins was a London typefounder, and sometime Sheriff of London and
Middlesex. Clement was a practising surgeon, a former Mayor of Shrewsbury,
a J.P. and Deputy Lieutenant of Merioneth, and the patron of a living.

Selected categories	Clement	Crawford	Figgins
Turnkeys	2	0	9
Sweeps	4	4	0
Clergymen	1	0	4
Organist	0	0	1
Sexton	0	0	1
Vestry clerk	1	0	1
Postman and P.O. clerks*	6	0	12
Dissenting ministers	8	6	0
Bankers	3	0	3
Farmers	6	1	7
Gentlemen	77	10	71
Surgeons	13	2	16
Lawyers	17	0	22
Victuallers	57	9	65
Beersellers	17	7	19
Printers	23	10	25
Shoemakers	101	50	92
Tailors	84	47	57
Carpenters	60	37	43
Grocers	23	6	18
Butchers	25	8	28
Railwaymen	73	38	58
Labourers	131	85	147

Plumps		Splits	
Figgins	703	Clement and Figgins	1,047
Clement	147	Clement and Crawford	672
Crawford	30	Crawford and Figgins	2

* The postmaster plumped for Figgins.

The Shropshire election of 1831

An analysis of a Tory victory at the Reform general election of 1831 in the 'most Tory county in England'. The pollbook is in Manchester Reference Library.

Result:
Sir Rowland Hill, Tory	1,824
J. C. Pelham, Esq., Tory	1,355
William Lloyd, Whig	835
John Mytton, Whig	395

Voters A–G inclusive

Selected categories	Hill	Pelham	Lloyd	Mytton
Gentlemen	93	89	30	15
Farmers	230	175	84	46

The two Darbys of Coalbrookdale each split their votes between Lloyd and Mytton. Viscount Clive voted for Hill and Pelham.

All voters except farmers and gentlemen

	Hill	Pelham	Lloyd	Mytton
I. Clergymen	99	89	15	2
Parish clerks	74	67	10	7
Organist	1	1	0	0
Dissenting ministers*	0	0	2	1
II. Surgeons	18	10	10	2
Lawyers	13	12	8	2
Schoolmasters	15	9	4	1
Surveyor, auctioneer, bailiff, land agent	22	15	12	4
Vets., farriers	5	2	2	0
III. Bankers	11	9	3	0
Ironmasters	4	2	6	1
Builders	12	8	6	4
Innkeepers	60	38	33	20
Millers, maltsters	62	51	36	11
Brickmakers	8	4	2	1
Bargeowners	9	9	4	1
Merchants	16	7	16	3
IV. Butchers	41	30	23	18
Bakers	10	9	11	3
Chemists	3	2	4	1
Hairdressers	4	3	3	2
Ironmongers	12	6	12	2
Wine merchants	8	4	5	1
Booksellers	1	0	3	2
Drapers, glovers, hatters	21	17	21	8
Grocers and other shops	42	23	49	18

* The votes of three Dissenting ministers who wished to vote for Lloyd and Mytton were disallowed.

The Shropshire election of 1831 (cont.)

	Hill	Pelham	Lloyd	Mytton
V. Labourers	88	64	44	30
Weavers	4	3	2	2
Miners, colliers	11	7	10	2
Servants, gardeners	29	18	11	5
Carters	8	6	5	2
Miscellaneous	54	37	48	21
VI. Shoemakers	39	28	45	30
Tailors	22	15	22	14
Printers	4	1	2	0
Coopers	7	4	9	4
Blacksmiths	33	20	15	11
Plumbers	6	4	3	2
Building crafts	33	21	15	12
Brazier, tinman, white-smith, watchmaker	14	6	11	4
Saddlers	13	10	6	4
Tanners, Skinners	9	6	10	2
Cabinetmakers, upholsterers	12	6	6	5
Curriers	3	4	13	5
Joiners, carpenters, sawyers	33	30	22	17
Painters, glaziers	17	9	11	3
Wheelwrights	21	16	13	7

Plumps		Splits	
Hill	275	Hill and Pelham	1,268
Pelham	46	Lloyd and Mytton	285
Lloyd	267	Hill and Lloyd	251
Mytton	71	Hill and Mytton	30
		Pelham and Lloyd	32
		Pelham and Mytton	9

The Shropshire (North) election of 1832

The pollbook is in the Guildhall Library.

Result: Rowland Hill, Conservative	3,002
John Cotes, Liberal	2,104
Ormesby Gore, Conservative	2,032

Voters A–D inclusive: selected categories	Cotes	Hill	Gore
Clergymen	8	18	16
Dissenting minister	0	1	0
Ironmasters	3	0	2
Colliers	10	0	0
Parish clerks	4	5	4
Shoemakers	22	16	6
Gentlemen	27	47	36
Farmers	192	307	192
Labourers	45	54	29

The Southampton election of 1852

Result: B. M. Willcox, Liberal   1,058
Sir A. E. Cockburn, Liberal   1,012
A. B. Cochrane, Conservative   797
A. A. Vansittart, Conservative   770

Selected categories	Willcox	Cockburn	Cochrane	Vansittart
Dissenting ministers	4	4	0	0
R.N., all ranks	5	5	7	7
Army, all ranks	0	0	10	10
Bankers	2	2	0	0
Railway, all grades	16	15	5	4
Boilermakers	6	6	2	0
Anglican clergy	0	0	11	12
Servants	2	2	6	6
Police, all grades	5	5	0	1
Saddlers	4	4	2	2
Pilots	4	3	6	5
Sexton	0	0	1	1
Surgeons	10	9	9	10
Master mariners	4	3	4	3
Mariners	40	30	13	7
Labourers	27	27	11	11
Merchants	24	21	18	15
Sailmakers	2	2	4	4
Shipwrights	15	13	5	3

The Staffordshire (West) election of 1868

The pollbook is in Cambridge University Library.

Result: Smith Child, Conservative   3,909
H. F. M. Ingram, Conservative   3,773
W. O. Foster, Liberal   3,295
H. W. H. Foley, Liberal   3,244

Clergymen: for Ingram   60
for Child   60
for Foley   5
for Foster   6
Abstained   12 (mostly living at a distance)

The Stockport election of 1847

Result: Cobden, Liberal   643
James Heald, Tory   570
James Kershaw, Liberal   537
John West, Radical   14

All voters	Cobden	Kershaw	Heald
I. Gentlemen	15	13	20
Medical	6	4	10
Official	6	5	2
Other professions	7	9	20
Legal	7	5	9
	41	36	61

N

The Stockport election of 1847 (cont.)

All voters	Cobden	Kershaw	Heald
II. Textile workers	16	38	20
Cotton masters	13	14	8
Managers	38	27	32
	67	79	60
III. Butchers	15	14	15
Shopkeepers	151	135	111
	166	149	126
IV. Beersellers	24	29	18
Publicans	42	30	52
Brewers	0	0	4
	66	59	74
V. Building	8	6	11
Leather	0	6	6
Minor crafts	7	4	13
Metal	14	15	21
Wood	8	8	16
Tailors	14	11	9
Shoemakers	11	6	11
	62	56	87
VI. Dealers	32	26	37
Hat manufacturers	9	5	1
Minor manufacturers*	29	25	19
Builders	2	5	6
Farmers	6	3	6
	78	64	69
VII. Labourers	0	1	1
Servants, etc.	3	5	4
Clerks	10	11	9
Miscellaneous†	14	21	54
Carriers	2	0	5
	29	38	73

Summary	Cobden	Kershaw	Heald
I. Upper crust	41	36	61
II. Textile interest	67	79	60
III. Shopkeepers	166	149	126
IV. Drink	66	59	74
V. Craftsmen	62	56	87
VI. Small business	78	64	69
VII. Miscellaneous	29	38	73

* Mainly candlewick makers.   † Mainly outvoters.

No usable materials survive for the earlier elections, but there is a little further evidence that business was by no means always Liberal. Cobden, remarking that the millowners 'who neither changed their clothes nor closed their eyes for 36 hours' were working for him in 1841, stated 'these men were against me at the former election', i.e. they must have voted for an orthodox Tory candidate with strong local connections. See John Morley, *The Life of Richard Cobden* (1881), I, 176.

The Suffolk election of August 1830

The pollbook is in the Guildhall Library. It does not state the occupations of voters.

Result: Sir H. E. Bunbury, Bt., Whig   1,097
Chas. Tyrell, Whig   1,064
Sir T. S. Gooch, Bt., Tory   627

Bunbury was a Whig, and Tyrell a Whiggish Tory. Gooch, who had been returned for 25 years unopposed, was a thick and thin supporter of ministers.

	Bunbury	Tyrell	Gooch
Clergy	26	23	72
Dissenting ministers	3	3	0

The Suffolk West election of 1868

The pollbook is in the Guildhall Library.

Result: Major Windsor Parker, Conservative   2,500
Lord Augustus Hervey, Conservative   2,389
Charles Lamport, Liberal   1,704

Anglican clergy (distinguished by the prefix 'Rev.') voted as follows:

Lamport   3
Hervey   101
Parker   99

The Tamworth election of 1837

The pollbook is in the Guildhall Library.

Result: Sir Robert Peel, Conservative   387
Captain A'Court, R.N., Conservative   244
Captain Townshend, R.N., Liberal   186

Selected categories	Townshend	Peel	A'Court
Surgeons	1	4	3
Parish clerk	0	1	1
Butchers	4	12	8
Grocers	3	7	4
Shoemakers	17	20	5
Labourers	28	46	27
Innkeepers	11	29	19
Beersellers	1	2	2
Farmers	11	32	26
Town crier	0	1	1
R.C. priest	1	1	0
Woolstaplers	1	1	1
Miners	3	2	0
Coalmasters	0	2	1

The Tamworth election of 1841

The pollbook is in the Guildhall Library.

Result: Peel, Conservative   365
A'Court, Conservative   241
Townshend, Liberal   147

Selected categories	Townshend	Peel	A'Court
Solicitors	0	3	3
Surgeons	0	4	3
Parish clerks	0	1	1
Butchers	2	9	7
Grocers	1	11	7
Shoemakers	12	19	8
Labourers	27	47	23
Innkeepers	9	24	19
Beersellers	0	1	0
Farmers	9	32	28
Relieving officer	0	1	1
Organist	0	1	1
Dissenting minister	1	0	0
Town crier	0	1	1
Paper manufacturer	0	1	1
Canal agent	1	0	0
Woolstapler	1	0	0
Cotton spinners	0	2	2
Bleacher	0	1	1
Coalmaster	0	1	1
Tape manufacturers	1	2	2

The Tewkesbury election of May 1831

The pollbook is in the Guildhall Library.

Result: John Martin, Whig   238
J. E. Dowdeswell, Tory   222
C. H. Tracy, Whig   170

Resident voters

All voters	Martin	Tracy	Dowdeswell
Gentlemen	10	6	7
Stocking makers and weavers	13	8	7
Flax dresser	1	1	0
Wine merchants	1	0	3
Gardeners	2	1	1
Cabinet makers	3	2	1
Baker	1	1	0
Bookseller	0	1	1
Labourers, bargemen	10	8	1
Butchers	3	3	5

The Tewkesbury election of May 1831 (cont.)

All voters	Martin	Tracy	Dowdeswell
Grocers	3	4	1
Other shopkeepers	9	9	4
Lawyers	2	2	1
Innkeepers	7	3	7
Shoemakers	5	3	6
Farmers, yeomen	8	6	4
Gaoler	0	1	1
Dissenting ministers	1	2	0
Surgeon	0	0	1
Clergyman	0	0	1
Miscellaneous	46	36	24

Non-resident voters

All voters	Martin	Tracy	Dowdeswell
Innkeepers	2	1	3
Farmers, yeomen	14	11	36
Lawyers	5	3	9
Gentlemen	37	20	42
Butcher	1	1	0
Officers	0	0	3
Surgeons	5	3	5
Labourers	3	1	3
Shoemakers	2	2	0
Clergymen	4	3	16
Bankers	3	2	2
Merchant	0	0	1
Miscellaneous	37	27	25

Splits and plumps

Dowdeswell and Martin	77
Dowdeswell and Tracy	15
Martin and Tracy	151
Tracy alone	4
Martin alone	10
Dowdeswell alone	130

The Tewkesbury election of 1841

The pollbook is in the Guildhall Library.

Result: Wm. Dowdeswell, Conservative	193
John Martin, Liberal	189
John Easthope, Liberal	181

All voters	Martin	Easthope	Dowdeswell
Craftsmen	50	46	35
Farmers, yeomen	9	9	24
Labourers	2	2	3
Gentlemen	11	10	28

The Tewkesbury election of 1841 (cont.)

All voters	Martin	Easthope	Dowdeswell
Stocking makers	13	12	3
Innkeepers	6	6	16
Shoemakers	11	10	8
Lawyers	4	4	7
Butchers	2	1	4
Grocers	6	6	2
Beersellers	7	7	0
Surgeons	2	1	4
Baptist ministers	2	2	0
Independent minister	1	1	0
Gaoler	1	1	0

The Wakefield election of 1837

The pollbook is in the Guildhall Library.

Result: Hon. W. S. Lascelles, Conservative   307
D. Gaskell, Liberal   281

Selected categories	Gaskell	Lascelles
Innkeepers	23	29
Gentlemen	22	14
Lawyers	5	17
Clothiers	4	1
Butchers	9	9
Watermen	2	0
Shoemakers	12	7
Corn merchants	11	9
Beersellers	9	6
Minister	1	0
Woolstaplers	13	7
Grocers	9	8
Surgeons	5	11
Dyers	3	0
Merchants	2	2
Boilermaker	1	0
Engineer	1	0
Manufacturers	8	2
Farmers	1	2
Clergymen	3	6
Wharfingers	3	0
Bankers	1	1
Worsted spinners	2	6
Ironfounders	0	3
Registrar	0	1

The Warrington election of 1847

Result: G. Greenall, Protectionist 327
Wm. Allcard, Liberal   293

All voters	Allcard	Greenall		Allcard	Greenall
I. Gentlemen	13	14	Ironmasters	18	8
Farmers	8	50	Cottonmasters	9	0
II. Legal	1	10	Dealers and manufacturers	4	2
Medical	3	7			
Officials	0	5	VI. Labourers	10	17
Other professions	15	12	Textile workers	10	0
III. Publicans	29	40	Metal workers	25	9
IV. Clerks	9	20	VII. Butchers	4	11
V. Glass manufacturers	0	6	Drapers	9	10
Bankers	0	3	Other shopkeepers	74	40
Brewers	4	7	VIII. Tailor	4	5
Corn and flour	12	9	Shoemaker	9	4
Coal	0	2	Wood	9	14
Builders	2	0	Leather	6	5
			Others	10	12
			Painter	0	3

Summary:	Allcard	Greenall
I, II. Upper crust	40	98
III. Publicans	29	40
IV. Clerks	9	20
V. Business	49	37
VI. Labour	45	26
VII. Shopkeepers	87	61
VIII. Craftsmen	38	43

The Warwick Borough election of May 1831

The pollbook is in the Institute of Historical Research.

Result: John Tomes, Whig   698
Hon. Sir Chas. J. Greville, Tory   505
E. B. King, Whig   523

Selected categories	Greville	Tomes	King
Gentlemen	28	25	21
Bankers	3	1	1
Surgeons	6	6	4
Lawyers	5	7	7
Clergymen	3	1	0
Dissenting ministers	0	2	2
Turnkey	1	0	0
Millers	8	4	3

The Warwick Borough election of May 1831 (cont.)

Selected categories	Greville	Tomes	King
Farmers	34	11	4
Publicans	21	17	8
Woolcombers	1	15	15
Woolsorters	0	4	4
Woolstaplers	0	4	4
Butchers	18	16	13
Grocers	7	12	11
Carpenters	23	39	29
Tailors	23	35	28
Shoemakers	26	45	37
Labourers	47	73	64

Greville: splits	203	Tomes: splits	697
plumps	302	plumps	1

King: splits 518
plumps 5

The Wigan election of 31 July 1830*

The pollbook is in the Guildhall Library.

Result:	James Hardcastle, Radical	116
	Richard Potter, Radical	112
	J. A. Hodson, Tory	54
	Col. Jas. Lindsay, Tory	45
	J. H. Kearsley, Tory	12

(No parties given.)

All voters	Kearsley	Hodson	Lindsay	Potter	Hardcastle
Cotton spinners	3	5	3	3	3
Bankers	0	2	2	0	0
Gentlemen	4	19	16	6	6
Solicitors	0	3	1	2	4
Timber merchant	0	1	1	0	0
Yeomen	0	1	1	1	1
Cotton merchants	0	0	0	3	3
Farmers	0	2	1	0	1
Cordwainers	1	1	0	4	4
Iron merchants	0	1	2	0	0
Linen manufacturer	0	1	1	0	0
Linen merchant	0	1	1	0	0
Innkeepers	1	1	1	17	18
Butchers	0	3	3	2	2
Manufacturers	1	1	2	6	6
Surgeons	0	0	0	4	4
Tailors	0	0	0	6	6
Grocers	0	0	0	6	6
Divers other occupations	2	13	11	52	52

* The returning officers refused the votes of many legally qualified voters, hence statistics given by Bean, etc., differ wildly from the above.

The Yarmouth election of 1830

The pollbook is in King's Lynn Public Library.

Result: Hon. Col. G. Anson, Whig   946
C. E. Rumbold, Whig   945
T. E. Campbell, Tory   754
H. Preston, Tory   751

Residence of voter	Anson	Rumbold	Campbell	Preston
Yarmouth and Southtown	502	502	427	424
Norfolk	76	75	34	34
Norwich	51	51	44	44
Suffolk and Essex	67	67	67	67
London, Middlesex, Surrey	161	161	106	106
Kent	68	68	42	43
Distant voters	21	21	33	33
	946	945	753	751

Splits for Anson and Rumbold   942
Splits for Preston and Campbell   750

In-voters

Selected categories	Anson	Rumbold	Campbell	Preston
Parish clerk	0	0	1	1
Sexton	0	0	1	1
Publicans	1	1	5	5
Pilots	2	2	1	1
R.N. officers	1	1	5	5
Surgeons	2	2	8	8
Solicitors	7	7	7	7
Gentlemen	21	21	32	32
Merchants	12	12	18	18
Shipowners	6	6	2	2
Shipbuilders	1	1	3	3
Shipwrights	56	56	60	60
Mariners	82	82	62	61
Tailors	10	10	6	6
Cordwainers	16	16	5	5

Norfolk and Suffolk out-voters

Selected categories	Anson	Rumbold	Campbell	Preston
R.N. officers	0	0	3	3
Pilots	1	1	7	7
Surgeons	2	2	3	3
Solicitors	4	4	2	2
Gentlemen	21	21	20	20
Farmers	9	9	8	8
Shipwrights	11	11	12	12
Mariners	6	6	8	8
Tailors	7	7	1	1
Cordwainers	10	9	1	1

The Yarmouth election of 1830 (cont.)

London, Kent and distant places

Selected categories of out-voters	Anson	Rumbold	Campbell	Preston
R.N. officers	o	o	6	7
Pilot	1	1	o	o
Surgeons	2	2	2	2
Solicitors	1	1	5	5
Gentlemen	12	13	16	16
Shipwrights	69	69	32	32
Mariners	28	29	12	12
Tailors	6	6	6	6
Cordwainers	10	10	2	2

The Yarmouth election of December 1832

The pollbook is in the Institute of Historical Research.

Result: C. E. Rumbold, Liberal   837
Hon. Geo. Anson, Liberal   828
A. Colvile, Conservative   750

Plumps

Rumbold   o
Anson   7
Colvile   688

Selected categories	Anson	Rumbold	Colvile
Surgeons	7	7	8
Pilots	6	6	11
Parish clerk	o	o	1

The Yarmouth by-election of 1838

Result: Wm. Wilshere, Liberal   735
Thos. Baring, Conservative   702

Selected categories	Wilshere	Baring
Officers	4	o
Surgeons	5	15
Pilots	4	5
Parish clerks	o	2
Organist	1	o

The Yarmouth election of 1841

The pollbook is in the Institute of Historical Research.

Result: Wm. Wilshere, Liberal   945
C. E. Rumbold, Liberal   943
Thos. Baring, Conservative   501
J. Somes, Conservative   494

Freemen and householders together

Selected categories	Wilshere	Rumbold	Baring	Somes
Officers	6	6	0	0
Mariners	59	59	15	14
Shipwrights	82	84	65	62
Sailmakers	16	15	9	10
Caulkers	27	26	7	6
Fishermen	7	6	5	5
Pilots	2	2	8	8

£10 householders only

Selected categories	Wilshire	Rumbold	Baring	Somes
Surgeons	3	3	5	5
Grocers	16	16	1	1
Butchers	7	6	2	2

The Yarmouth election of 1847

The pollbook is in the Institute of Historical Research.

Result: Lord A. Lennox, Conservative   834
Octavius Coope, Conservative   813
C. E. Rumbold, Liberal   729
Francis Goldsmid, Liberal   698

Freemen voters only:

selected categories	Rumbold	Goldsmid	Lennox	Coope
Gentlemen	25	25	27	25
Surgeons	4	2	4	5
Solicitors	11	11	8	8
Cordwainers	20	22	17	19
Grocers	5	5	6	6
Tailors	12	12	13	13
Publicans	5	5	9	8
Mariners	46	45	62	62
Shipwrights	34	39	62	59
Pilots	1	1	7	7

Freemen electors   918
£10 householders   644
Total poll   1,562

The York City election of 1835

The pollbook is in the Guildhall Library.

Result: Lowther, Conservative   1,499
Dundas, Liberal   1,301
Barkley, Liberal   919

Selected categories	Dundas	Barkley	Lowther
Watermen	1	1	14
Policemen	3	2	0
Chorister	0	0	1
Organist	0	0	1
Gentlemen	99	55	100
Surgeons	14	7	19
Farmers	1	0	0
Shoemakers	127	104	124
Weavers	7	7	4
Grocers	1	0	1
Butchers	38	25	61
Labourers	23	8	49
Dissenting ministers	3	3	0

The York City election of 1841

The pollbook is in the Bodleian Library.

Result: Lowther, Conservative   1,625
Yorke, Liberal   1,552
Atcherley, Conservative   1,456

Voters A–G inclusive only

Selected categories	Yorke	Lowther	Atcherley
Stonemasons	9	5	3
Grocers	7	9	8
Butchers	11	27	27
Shoemakers	57	42	37
Farmers	13	33	28
Labourers	13	14	11

Voters A–Z

Selected categories	Yorke	Lowther	Atcherley
Surgeons	16	20	20
Merchants	4	0	0
Basketmakers	3	6	5
Saddlers	15	18	13
Comb makers	52	33	31
Clergy	4	23	23
Wesleyan ministers	0	3	3
Weavers	17	8	6

The York City election of 1841 (cont.)

Voters A–Z *(cont.)*

Selected categories	Yorke	Lowther	Atcherley
Railwaymen	1	2	2
Proctors	1	4	4
Choristers	0	3	3
Organbuilders	2	4	3
Organist	0	1	1
Vestry clerk	0	1	1
Policemen	1	4	3
Dissenting ministers	2	0	0
Sexton	0	1	1
Unitarian minister	1	0	0

The York City election of 1852

The pollbook is in the Institute of Historical Research.

Result: J. G. Smyth, Conservative　1,870
W. M. E. Milner, Liberal　1,831
Henry Vincent, Chartist　886

Selected categories	Vincent	Milner	Smyth
Railway employees, all grades	4	18	38
Watermen	2	7	14
Policemen	0	5	5
Dissenting ministers	0	3	0
Clergymen	0	1	3
Vergers	0	1	3
Chorister	0	0	1
Organist	0	0	1
Bankers	0	2	3
Gentlemen	24	99	141
Lawyers	2	25	34
Surgeons	0	12	24
Farmers	9	46	60
Publicans	12	56	52
Shoemakers	80	94	96
Curriers	9	25	30
Tailors	56	52	57
Weavers	5	10	7
Grocers	11	26	21
Butchers	19	70	72
Labourers	21	33	43

Plumps		Splits	
Smyth	969	Smyth and Milner	881
Milner	563	Smyth and Vincent	20
Vincent	479	Milner and Vincent	387

BIBLIOGRAPHY

A. SOCIOLOGICAL THEORY AND SOCIAL STRUCTURE

Bellerby, J. R. 'Distribution of Manpower in Agriculture and Industry 1851–1951', *Farm Economist*, IX (1958).

Booth, Charles. 'Occupations of the People of the United Kingdom, 1801–1881', *Journal of the Statistical Society*, XLIX (June 1886), 314–44.

Clapham, J. H. *An Economic History of Modern Britain: Free Trade and Steel 1850–1886*. [There is a table of occupations drawn from the 1851 census on page 23.]

Dahrendorf, Ralf. *Class and Class Conflict in Industrial Society*. London, 1959.

Day, Clive. 'The Distribution of Industrial Occupations in England, 1841–1861', *Transactions of the Connecticut Academy* (1927).

Hirsch, G. P. 'The Size of Farm Holdings in England and Wales', *Farm Economist*, IX (1958), 87.

Report of Departmental Committee on Factory Statistics: *Parl. Papers* (1895), XIX, 583.

Return of all persons employed coming under all Factories and Workshops Acts. *Parl. Papers* (1871), LXII, 164.

Routh, G. G. C. *Occupation and Pay in Great Britain, 1906–60* (1965).

Tawney, A. J. and Tawney, R. H. 'An Occupational Census of the Seventeenth Century', *Economic History Review*, V (1934–5), 25.

B. POLLBOOKS

British Museum. The Museum has a handlist, kept at the counter, of its holdings of pollbooks.

Camps, Anthony J. *Poll Books: a list of those in the Library of the Society of Genealogists*, 1961.

Cannon, John. 'Short Guides to Records: 2. Poll Books', *History* (June 1962).

History of Parliament Trust. *Draft Register of Pollbooks*. 21 Oct. 1953. [This is a list of some 1,750 pollbooks printed between 1694 and 1882, based on exhaustive enquiries in libraries all over the country.]

McCalmont, H. *Parliamentary Pollbook*. London, 1910.

Smith, Henry Stooks. *The Register of Parliamentary Contested Elections*. London, 1841.